ANTI-INFLAMMATORY DIET FOR BEGINNERS

1500 Days of Easy and Tasty Recipes to Heal the Immune System, Reduce your Body Inflammation, and Balance Hormones. Includes 30-Day Meal Plan

Laura Kelley

ISBN: 979-8351122847
10 9 8 7 6 5 4 3 2 1

Laura Kelley
HEALTHY FOOD FOR HEALTHY BODIES

GET YOUR BONUS NOW!

Hello! First of all, I would like to thank you for purchasing "Anti-Inflammatory Cookbook for Beginners." I'm sure it will be very useful to improve your eating habits and overall well-being!.
To prove my gratitude for the trust you have placed in my experience, I am so happy to gift you with another one of my books, "The Whole Body Reset Cookbook,"
which I am sure will make your health explode. Don't wait any longer, follow the instructions below to download the digital version for free! Enjoy your reading!

The Whole Body Reset Cookbook
1500-Day Easy and Tasty Recipes to Live Healthier in Your Midlife and Beyond. Boost Your Metabolism and Achieve a Flat Belly in Just 15 Days. Includes 30-Day Meal Plan

The bonus is **100% free**, with no strings attached.
You don't need to enter any details except your name and email address.

To download your bonuses scan the QR code below or go to

https://books-bonuses.com/laura-kelley-bonuses

Table of Contents

Introduction

An anti-inflammatory diet is a diet that provides the best balance of vitamins, minerals, and essential nutrients for optimum health. It reduces symptoms of inflammation in your body by preventing the build-up of free radicals. Some foods can cause inflammation in your body. However, eating an anti-inflammatory diet is healthier and safer for your body. For some people, certain food groups (such as dairy products and gluten) are so problematic that they don't consume them at all. Others may seek to avoid them if possible.

An anti-inflammatory diet gives you a better quality of life by reversing the symptoms of chronic illnesses. It is based on your needs, whether you want to lose weight or live a healthy lifestyle. The cure for chronic inflammation may not be a pill but changes in diet and lifestyle. An anti-inflammatory diet helps you lose weight and improve your health naturally.

The book contains 120 delicious, easy and healthy recipes to try. You will see significant changes in your diet plan by following the recipes in this cookbook. Everything you need is right here in this cookbook to achieve better health. All the meals are easy to prepare and are very nutritious. It will help you feel satisfied, energetic and focused on your daily tasks.

The anti-inflammatory diet helps you reduce the signs and symptoms of inflammation in your body healthier. It is not only used to cure chronic diseases, but it also allows you to achieve better health. The anti-inflammatory food plan includes all the necessary nutrients to achieve a healthy lifestyle. Chronic inflammation is not always a result of an autoimmune condition though usually, it is the cause of some illnesses and diseases such as lupus, rheumatoid arthritis, diabetes etc. Inflammation can be controlled by following the diet plan and even without any medication if you follow the diet plan consistently.

The anti-inflammatory diet contains a combination of foods, such as fish, legumes and vegetables, that help you achieve your goal of better health. It is used to cure chronic inflammation and reduce the risk of getting some chronic illnesses and diseases. An anti-inflammatory diet is designed to give you better health and gives you a way to get things under control so that you can have a healthier lifestyle.

This anti-inflammatory diet cookbook is designed to give you some delicious recipes that are easy enough for anyone to prepare, regardless of their cooking expertise.

The recipes in this book are successful, tasty and healthy simultaneously. The recipes are easy to prepare and a great addition to your everyday diet plan.

All the recipes in this book are made from natural food ingredients so that you can know what you are eating. Many people have tested the recipes, which were excellent with significant health benefits.

The ingredients used in these recipes can be easily purchased from the local supermarket or any other supermarket.

What is Anti-Inflammatory Diet

Inflammation is the body's natural reaction to infections, injuries, and illnesses. Common inflammation symptoms are redness, pain, heat, and swelling. Nevertheless, some diseases don't occur any symptoms. Such illnesses are diabetes, heart disease, cancer, etc. That's why we should care about our health permanently and stay a healthy lifestyle to live healthier or even longer.

The anti-inflammatory diet helps to reduce the level of free radicals in our bodies. The most common question is what to eat while on an anti-inflammatory diet. As usual, the diet is varied and includes many fruits, vegetables, whole grains, plant-based proteins (legumes and nuts), fatty types of fish, and a lot of spices, condiments, and dressings. The only condition that should be followed is that all food should be organic.

The most popular vegetables and fruits while the anti-inflammatory diet, is leafy greens, cherries, raspberries, blackberries, tomatoes, cucumbers, etc. If we talk about whole grains, these are oatmeal, brown rice, and all grains that are high in fiber. Natural herbs and spices are full of antioxidants that boost the health and taste of your food.

You should avoid highly processed food (sugary drinks, chocolate, ice cream, French fries, burgers, sausages, and deli meats) and overly greasy food during the diet. Another factor that will help you is the correct amount of water consumed daily. It is easy to count.

There are a lot of apps that will help you to do it correctly.

By drinking enough water, our bodies will cleanse faster.

As you noticed, the anti-inflammatory diet is simple to follow and is not strict. You are free to adjust the diet by your preferences.

The anti-inflammatory diet can be expensive as it emphasizes eating only organic food. Likewise, the diet contains a lot of allergens, such as nuts, seeds, and soy.

However, eating the right adjusted food will help eliminate the diet's cons. It is highly recommended to consult the doctor and complete a medical examination before starting the diet.

This is the essential information that you should know before starting a diet. Any diet is not a magic remedy for all diseases; it can support the body during a difficult treatment time. Start your new healthy life with a tiny step and you will see tremendous results within half a year. You can be sure that your body will be thankful for giving you a fresh look and energy for new achievements.

Symptoms of Chronic Inflammation

There are many symptoms of the condition. But they will always differ for each person, and the intensity will also vary. Here are some of the most common symptoms.

Fatigue – If you are constantly feeling tired, without any real reason, it could be because of chronic inflammation. This could be a sign that your body is battling out something. With inflammation, your body will ask for more cellular energy so that the immune cells can be regenerated. This will further deplete the necessary fuel your body needs, thus making you feel even more tired.

First, make sure that you are getting adequate sleep. You should be concerned if you are feeling tired even after this.

Physical Pains – Do you suffer from frequent pains and aches? Chronic pain can signify that you may have arthritis, which majorly contributes to inflammation. Body pains like joint and muscle aches are often caused by systematic inflammation. High levels of inflammatory cytokines in the body can attack joints and muscles, causing swelling, pain, and redness.

Skin Rashes – Rashes on the skin, like psoriasis or eczema, are inflammatory skin issues characterized by rough, flaky, and red skin. Psoriasis and eczema have both been linked to a hypersensitive immune system. Those who suffer from these conditions have more inflammatory mast cells that can trigger skin rashes when activated.

Even an acne breakout or too dry skin could signify chronic inflammation.

Excess Mucus – Feeling like blowing your nose or clearing your throat too often? It could be a sign that your body is inflamed. If the body feels it is inflamed, your mucous membranes will make thick phlegm to protect the epithelial cells in the lining of your respiratory system. This can cause a runny nose, sneezing, and constant coughing.

Digestive Issues – Constipation, abdominal pain, loose stool, and bloating are common digestive problems for many people. Chronic inflammation could be causing them. It can contribute to the leaking gut syndrome or permeability in the intestines that may cause toxins and bacteria to leak through the walls of your intestine to the rest of your body.

Be careful if you have a leaky gut because it can fuel systematic inflammation and cause digestive issues like irregular bowel movements and abdominal distention.

Heartburn – Be careful with heartburn as well. Clinical studies have revealed that GERD (Gastroesophageal Reflux Disease) is probably more from inflammation. Previously, it was believed that stomach acids traveling up from the esophagus were the cause of heartburn.

This study found that the human body's inflammatory response was causing pain and damage in the esophagus, eventually causing heartburn. Further, treating the inflammation resulted in a reduction in heartburn. The Journal of the American Medical Association published the findings of this study.

Swollen Lymph Nodes – The lymph nodes are primarily located in the neck region, close to the groin, and below the armpits. They can swell up if there is a physical problem in the body. So, it is essential to look out for them. They will swell if the body is battling against infection and then return to normal once we are well again.

If these nodes are constantly inflamed, then it could be a sign of a constant struggle. It could be a symptom of an underlying issue or a chronic illness.

Health Risks of Chronic Inflammation

Chronic inflammation may be fatal; according to estimates, 3 out of 5 individuals lose their lives due to inflammatory disorders. There are many health risks posed by inflammation, mainly including the following.

1. **Rheumatoid Arthritis:**

Let's say that inflammation makes arthritis almost unbearable. A person feels hampered in his movements, and sometimes it even hurts while talking and eating. The persistent state of swelling in the joints may result in permanent tissue damage to the patient. Patients of arthritis are therefore advised to keep this inflammation in check and continuously look for measures to control it.

2. Psoriasis:

It is another immune-mediated disease in which the patient may suffer from large patches of inflammation over the skin. It causes redness and itchiness on the skin and typically appears on the elbows, scalp, and knees. The swelling may increase if the problem is not timely dealt with.

3. Asthma:

Asthma is a respiratory condition in which the internal lining of the human respiratory system swells, constricts the air pathways, and leads to shortness of breath. A chronic state of asthma can even be fatal for the patients. Instant anti-inflammatory measures are required to treat this condition, but the patients are also advised to avoid consuming all such items which could trigger this reaction.

4. Inflammatory Bowel Disease:

Also known as Crohn's disease, in this condition, the inflammation occurs inside the digestive tract and swells the internal lining of the intestines. It causes pain in bowel movements, fatigue, diarrhea, and even weightlessness. Controlling the inflammation can prevent intense pain and discomfort in this disease.

5. Diabetes:

Inflammation can lead to insulin resistance, prediabetes, and ultimately to diabetes. The pancreatic inflammation can cause damage to the insulin-producing beta cells, eventually leading to diabetes. Diabetic patients should remain extra cautious of cell or tissue damage as their bodies may not respond well to the injuries.

6. Obesity:

Obesity and inflammation are closely linked to one another. Cronin inflammation may result in alleviating the rate of metabolism, and it may lead to unnecessary deposition of fats. The fat cells may further contribute to more inflammation, so the cycle continues. Before it gets critical, both obesity and inflammation should be dealt with.

7. **Heart Disease:**

Any obstruction in the blood flow eventually affects the functioning of the cardiac muscles. Inflammation can often constrict the blood vessels and leads to higher pressure inside. It, in turn, affects the heart and may lead to minor or permanent damages.

Common Chronic Inflammation Treatments

Whenever you injure yourself, you put an ice pack on it, apply pressure, or take some anti-inflammatory medication that will help you feel better in a day or two. Chronic inflammation, on the other hand, requires more long-term treatment.

1. **Medication**

While you can use non-steroidal anti-inflammatory (NSAID) pills, like ibuprofen, to alleviate some of the pain, these drugs have adverse side effects that make them an unrealistic option for long-term treatment. NSAIDs can cause cardiovascular issues, stomach ulcers, and kidney toxicity. This is especially true if you're elderly.

Then there are corticosteroids—one of the most effective medicines to treat chronic inflammation. They work by suppressing the genes that cause the inflammatory response. Of course, this medication isn't risk-free. It can cause high blood sugar, osteoporosis, slow wound healing, thinning skin, and more.

Considering that the available medication may cure your chronic inflammation but cause various other health issues, changing your diet may be the most effective way to handle it.

For example, eating or drinking something as familiar as turmeric can combat the inflammation in your body.

So, let's look at some other dietary changes that can help.

2. **Diet**

The best way to treat chronic inflammation is to change what you eat.

The main focus should be on consuming foods that reduce inflammation. On the flip side, if these foods are strangers to your stomach, your inflammation will worsen.

Eating the right foods, however, isn't as easy as it sounds. I know when I first attempted the anti-inflammatory diet, I quickly discovered that the world is geared toward convenience and not nutrition. It took me a really long time to learn to avoid the pre-packed, processed food aisles and go to the grocery store's fresh produce and wholesome side. Don't worry, though! You will overcome the American diet's curse with practice and determination.

Here's a list of foods you'll be enjoying plenty of thanks to their high antioxidant and polyphenol content.

- Tomatoes
- Leafy greens like kale and spinach
- Olive oil
- Fish
- Nuts
- Fruits

3. Lifestyle Changes

There's a reason why doctors tell you to exercise, relieve stress, and eat healthily—the effect it has on your health is undeniable.

Stress is part of life, but when you don't deal with it, your body loses the ability to manage the release of cortisol, leading to increased inflammation.

Sleep is one way to manage your stress levels. It gives your body time to rest and repair. People who don't sleep enough not only have elevated cortisol levels but will also suffer from chronic inflammation and other health problems.

Another way to beat stress is to get moving. Exercise significantly reduces inflammation and improves your overall well-being. Better yet, you only need to exercise for five days at a moderate intensity for 30 minutes, or 1 hour and 15 minutes at a high intensity three times a week.

It's also good to keep in mind that smoking and excessive alcohol consumption won't have a positive impact on the inflammation in your body. Quitting these habits is recommended.

One of the most impactful lifestyle changes you can make is to follow a diet geared toward reducing inflammation in your body. Unfortunately, the standard American diet has adversely affected our bodies. These packaged foods are so heavily processed they contain mountains of sodium and unhealthy fats—ingredients known for promoting inflammation.

On the other hand, the anti-inflammatory diet heavily focuses on eating unprocessed foods known for their antioxidant qualities. Following this diet, you can expect to experience:

- Fewer symptoms are associated with diseases caused by chronic inflammation.
- Improved blood sugar levels.
- Higher energy levels.
- A more stable mood.

Getting Into the Anti-Inflammatory Diet

It's essential that you don't become overwhelmed when embarking on an anti-inflammatory diet. Here are four easy dietary guidelines to focus on as you begin your journey.

Provide your body with unprocessed, nutrient-dense, healing foods that protect against inflammation.

Choose antioxidant-rich organic produce; wild-caught, cold-water fish high in omega-3 fatty acids; grass-fed, antibiotic-free meat and animal products; nuts and seeds high in healthy fats, protein, and fiber; and alliums (onions, garlic, leeks) and herbs (basil, oregano, rosemary) packed with unique inflammation-fighting compounds.

Avoid highly reactive foods that cause inflammation.

Not everyone will have the same foods that trigger imbalance in the body. Still, a few common ones tend to inflame all of us to one degree or another, including wheat gluten, processed dairy, refined sugar, peanuts, processed corn, soy, feedlot animal products, caffeine, and alcohol.

Some people are also sensitive to citrus fruits and produce in the nightshade family (such as tomatoes, potatoes, peppers, and eggplant), although these foods are otherwise generally beneficial.

Add supplements and spices that combat inflammation.

When buying supplements, choose natural, food-based ones that will be absorbed by your body more efficiently. Fermented cod liver oil is the perfect inflammation-fighting supplement. It's one of nature's richest sources of omega-3 fatty acids.

Anti-inflammatory spices, such as ginger, garlic, cinnamon, and turmeric, are lovely additions to meals, or you can purchase them in capsule form as a whole food supplement. Each contains unique and potent compounds. For example, garlic contains high levels of sulfur, which encourages the immune system to fight disease.

Focus on gut healing.

Take a supplemental probiotic—a substance that promotes the health and growth of beneficial intestinal flora (good bacteria naturally present in your intestines).

Choose one that contains several strains of bacteria in several billion CFUs (colony-forming units). Such a supplement is frequently needed because many things we ingest today kill these good bacteria, including NSAIDs (nonsteroidal anti-inflammatory drugs), birth control substances, antibiotics, and many processed foods.

Sip on bone broth containing amino acids that soothe and heal your gut's lining. Enjoy an array of fermented foods (such as sauerkraut, kimchi, traditionally fermented pickles, cultured yogurt, kombucha, and kefir) that deliver healthy gut bacteria straight to your digestive tract.

Anti-Inflammatory Diet Food List

1. Foods to Eat

Have you ever taken antihistamines? What do those medicines do? They instantly relieve the immune system and treat inflammation. The agents responsible for such relief can also be consumed through our food. Except that food does not carry any harm or side effects.

Dark Leafy Greens, Including Kale And Spinach:

All leafy and green vegetables contain antioxidants that support the immune system and relieve it. These vegetables can be consumed in meals or through regular drinks and beverages. For instance, a warming spinach soup or a kale smoothie can be an excellent option to treat your inflammation.

Leafy greens are so enriched with antioxidants that their contents are extracted for medicinal use. Avoid overcooking to preserve the natural constituents of these vegetables.

Blueberries, Blackberries, And Cherries:

In fruits, berries from that food group are recommended since they contain lots of antioxidants and lesser carbs and calories. Among all the fruits, berries are most recommended for an anti-inflammatory diet. They can be taken in desserts or snacks and smoothies. Regular use of berries can even prevent the usual puffiness of the face and hands.

Dark Red Grapes:

The dark red grapes contain resveratrol, a phytonutrient known for boosting the immune system, preventing prostate cancer, and relieving inflammation. The red or dark skin grapes are due to the presence of this anti-inflammatory agent. Reasonable consumption of red grapes is therefore highly recommended on this diet.

Vegetables, Such As Broccoli And Cauliflower:

The non-nightshade vegetables which do not carry solanine are also recommended for this diet. These veggies are nutrient-dense and do not carry any element which could trigger inflammation. Cauliflower, broccoli, mushrooms, yams, and sweet potatoes all are allowed on this diet.

Beans And Lentils:

Both beans and lentils are high in fiber and antioxidants, which makes them suitable ingredients for this diet. Kidney beans, chickpeas, brown lentils, and white beans all are ideal for reducing inflammation.

Green Tea:

Green tea contains flavonoids, which are another type of phytonutrient and carry antioxidant properties. Green tea brings relief to all sorts of inflammation. It is recommended for regular use to avoid swelling. It can either be consumed directly or by adding sugar-free drinks and juices.

Avocado And Coconut:

Both avocado and coconut are incredibly soothing in their properties. They carry all such antioxidants, which effectively reduce inflammation. Coconut water, flesh, milk, and cream are suitable for this diet.

Olives And Olive Oil:

Adding enough olives to the diet brings several nutrients and antioxidants. If you cannot always consume olives in your diet, then use olive oil in your cooking. A drizzle of olive oil to every salad and serving gives them a boost of phytonutrients.

Walnuts, Pistachios, Pine Nuts, And Almonds:

Nuts and seeds are considered significant for human health and metabolism. They carry essential oils and a concentrated sum of antioxidants. Nuts-based milk is an excellent choice for an anti-inflammatory diet.

Cold-Water Fish, Including Salmon And Sardines:

Seafood contains omega 3, along with other essential nutrients. Salmon and sardine are recommended to reduce inflammation.

Dark Chocolate:

Yes! Dark chocolate is a natural relief of swelling and pain. Chocolate can regulate the release of hormones in the body, supports the immune system, and strengthens it.

Spices And Herbs:

Turmeric, cinnamon, thyme, rosemary, parsley, oregano, basil, etc., all such spices and herbs contain anti-inflammatory agents in high amounts, so much that turmeric is even used in skin ointments to treat injuries or burns.

2. Foods to Avoid

Regarding any health-oriented diet, the focus should always remain on what to avoid. Here is the list of the ingredients which directly or indirectly contribute to the factors responsible for inflammation.

Omega 6 Fatty Acids:

The Omega 6 fatty acids in wide-ranging foods are essential for the human body. They are responsible for producing inflammatory chemicals once digested. The same fatty acids regulate metabolism, maintain bone health, and enhance the brain's functionality. Therefore, they cannot be avoided altogether. However, by creating the right balance between the intake of Omega-3 and Omega-6 fatty acids, a person can control the risk of inflammation. There are certain food items which are rich in Omega-6 fatty acids, so they should be avoided or consumed in a limited amount on an anti-inflammatory diet:

- Meat
- All dairy products, including milk, ice cream, cheese, and butter.
- Margarine.
- Most vegetable oils include cottonseed oil, peanut, corn, safflower, and soybean oil.

Processed Meats:

All processed food items, especially meat, are strictly forbidden in this diet as they may contain preservatives and amino acids, which directly lead to inflammation or the production of histamines.

Sugar And Sugary Drinks

Sugar is the primary stimulant of inflammation. Excessive glucose excites the cells and triggers the immune system to respond aggressively to all metabolic processes in the body. This regressive response may lead to excessive inflammation. Cut down on white sugar, brown sugar, and all sugary items from your diet and add low-carb sweeteners instead.

Trans Fats And Fried Foods

Trans fats are processed and hydrogenated artificially, which makes them even more harmful than naturally existing saturated fats. Food cooked in these trans fats is equally health-damaging. Steamed, smoked, and grilled food is a better and safer option for the anti-inflammatory diet.

Gluten, White Bread, And Pasta

Refined carbs are as health-damaging as sugar. And gluten can trigger specific allergies, which leads to inflammation. Therefore, gluten and all the items carrying gluten should be avoided in this diet plan, whether it may take its white bread or pasta. Instead, use nut-based flours like flaxseed meals, almond flour or coconut flour, and pasta made of gluten-free ingredients.

Processed Snack Foods

Snack food items are a Big NO GO for an anti-inflammatory diet and apparent reasons. These items are made out of all the raw ingredients which aggravate inflammation. It is better to replace them with a bowl of berries and a fruity smoothie.

Desserts:

Desserts contain sugars, refined flour, and gluten; all these ingredients contribute to inflammation. Therefore, they should be avoided. You can always make sugar-free, low-carb varieties of these desserts at home using the recipes discussed in the book's later sections. Be wise to look for better alternatives and bring health-friendly options into your life.

Excess Alcohol:

Excessive alcohol, like sugar, can contribute to inflammation. It is responsible for disrupting the natural metabolic processes, which lead to many problems, including swelling.

CHAPTER 1: Breakfasts

1. Banana Pancakes With Apricots

Preparation time: 5 minutes
Cooking time: 10 minutes
Servings: 8
Ingredients:

- 3 tablespoons of banana flour
- 3 tablespoons + 1 teaspoon of ghee
- 1 avocado
- 1 pinch of salt
- 1 teaspoon of turmeric powder
- 1 cup unsweetened coconut milk
- 5 pitted apricots

Directions:

1. Combine the banana flour with the salt and turmeric powder.
2. In another bowl, combine the 3 tablespoons of ghee with the peeled and pitted avocado and mash with a fork.
3. Combine the two preparations and add the coconut milk slowly, stirring constantly.
4. Spread the dough with a spoon on a baking sheet covered with parchment paper, forming circles.
5. Bake in a hot oven at 360° F for about 10 minutes.
6. While the pancakes are cooking, cut the apricots into cubes and brown them for 5 minutes in a pan with a teaspoon of ghee.
7. Serve pancakes with the apricot compote.

Per serving: Calories: 129kcal; Fat: 11g; Protein: 1g; Carbs: 10g

2. Pudding With Blackcurrant And Mint

Preparation time: 3 minutes + 1 night rest
Cooking time: 5 minutes
Servings: 4
Ingredients:

- 1 cup unsweetened coconut milk
- 2 tablespoons of ground Chia seeds
- 1 teaspoon of vanilla extract
- 1 pinch of salt
- 1 cup of blackcurrant
- 2 teaspoons of raw honey
- 5 fresh mint leaves
- 2 tablespoons of water

Directions:

1. Combine the almond milk with the chia seeds, and add the vanilla extract and salt.
2. Pour the mixture into small glasses and let it rest in the refrigerator overnight.
3. In the morning, mix the honey with the water and put it in a non-stick pan with the currants. Cook for 5 minutes.
4. Pour the cooked currants over the puddings, which will have thickened overnight, decorate with mint leaves and enjoy.

Per serving: Calories: 85kcal; Fat: 3g; Protein: 3g; Carbs: 15g

3. Quinoa Bread With Pecan Walnut Butter

Preparation time: 15 minutes + 3 hours of rest
Cooking time: 30 minutes
Servings: 15
Ingredients:

- 3 cups of pecan nuts with pellicle
- 1 ½ cups of hazelnuts
- 6 drops of sage essential oil for food (or 1 tablespoon of sage powder)
- 4 cups of quinoa flour
- 1 dose of organic dry yeast
- 1 + 1/3 cup of water
- 2 tablespoons of olive oil

Directions:

1. Place the pecans, hazelnuts, salt and sage essential oil in the blender after lightly toasting them in the oven at 350° F for 5 minutes.
2. Continue to blend until the nuts release their natural oil, blend until creamy, and add water if necessary. Sage essential oil has a purifying power.
3. If you don't have it, replace it with powdered sage.
4. The bread: mix the quinoa flour with the organic yeast and salt.
5. Slowly add the oil and incorporate the water, preferably lukewarm, into the mixture.
6. Work it with your hands until you get a smooth ball.
7. Let it rise for at least 3 hours in a dark place, sheltered from drafts and warm.
8. Bake in a hot oven at 360° F for about 30 minutes. This bread is very dry and crunchy, perfect for nut butter.
9. Nut butter can be stored in an airtight food container in the refrigerator for at least a week.

Per serving: Calories: 144kcal; Fat: 4g; Protein: 5g; Carbs: 22g

4. Oat Flakes With Pears And Blueberries

Preparation time: 3 minutes
Cooking time: 10 minutes
Servings: 2
Ingredients:

- 2/3 cup of rolled oats
- 2 cups unsweetened almond milk
- 1 pinch of salt
- 1/4 cup of blueberries
- 1 pear
- 1 teaspoon of ground cinnamon
- 1 teaspoon of ground ginger
- 1 teaspoon of powdered mint

Directions:

1. Bring the almond milk, salt, cinnamon, ginger and mint to a boil in a saucepan. Lower the heat to a minimum and add the oats. Cook for about 10 minutes.
2. Serve the oats with fresh blueberries and pear.
3. If you prefer a scorching meal, heat the blueberries and pear in a teaspoon of ghee.

Per serving: Calories: 166kcal; Fat: 5g; Protein: 5g; Carbs: 27g

5. Soy Cream With Asparagus

Preparation time: 3 minutes
Cooking time: 10 minutes
Servings: 3
Ingredients:

- 1 cup unsweetened natural soy yogurt
- 2 tablespoons of ground flaxseed
- 1 teaspoon of coconut oil
- 11 ounces of asparagus
- 1 pinch of salt

Directions:

1. Cook the asparagus in the steamer.
2. If you do not have the steamer, boil the asparagus in a pan of lightly salted water for 10 minutes.
3. Drain them well and cut them into small pieces.
4. Put the yogurt in a bowl, add the ground flax seeds and mix well.
5. Add the asparagus and season with the olive oil.

Per serving: Calories: 156kcal; Fat: 11g; Protein: 8g; Carbs: 10g

6. Millet Cake With Plums

Preparation time: 10 minutes
Cooking time: 30 minutes
Servings: 10
Ingredients:

- 2 cups of millet
- 4 cups of water
- 1 cup of rolled oats
- 10 pitted dried plums
- 2 fresh organic eggs
- 1 pinch of salt

Directions:

1. Put the plums in a bowl of cold water and let them rest for 20 minutes.
2. Cook the millet in 4 cups of water, and add a pinch of salt and prunes.
3. Remove from the heat and allow to cool. Add the beaten eggs, mix carefully and bake in a preheated oven at 400° F for 30 minutes.

Per serving: Calories: 100kcal; Fat: 18g; Protein: 3g; Carbs: 18g

7. Crepes Of Chickpeas And Spinach

Preparation time: 10 minutes + 2 hours of rest
Cooking time: 15 minutes
Servings: 4
Ingredients:

- 1 cup of chickpea flour
- 1 cup of water
- 1 pinch of salt
- 2 tablespoons of olive oil
- 1 cup of spinach

Directions:

1. In a non-stick pan, cook the spinach with a tablespoon of olive oil. If necessary, add a few tablespoons of water.
2. Mix the chickpea flour with the water, salt and oil and leave to rest in the refrigerator for two hours.
3. Heat a non-stick pan and grease with a bit of oil. Pour a ladle of batter, and the dough will be distributed. Each spoon will be a crepe.
4. Fill the crepes with spinach.

Per serving: Calories: 121kcal; Fat: 5g; Protein: 6g; Carbs: 14g

8. Pistachio And Pecan Walnuts Granola For Breakfast

Preparation time: 10 minutes
Cooking time: 10 minutes
Servings: 13
Ingredients:

- 4 cups of oat flakes
- 1 ½ cups of dried figs
- 1/2 cup of coconut water
- 1 ½ cups of cashews
- 1 ½ cups of pecans with pellicle
- 1 pinch of salt

- 1 teaspoon ground cinnamon
- 1 teaspoon of raw cocoa powder

Directions:

1. Blend the dried figs with the coconut water in the food processor.
2. Coarsely chop the pecans and cashew nuts. Mix the cashews, pecans, date paste, cinnamon, salt and cocoa in a bowl. Heat the oven to 350° F.
3. Line a baking sheet with parchment paper. Pour the granola onto the pan, bake for 5 minutes, mix and bake for another 5 minutes.
4. This preparation is excellent in the morning with yogurt or to enrich ice cream and puddings.

Per serving: Calories: 259kcal; Fat: 19g; Protein: 5g; Carbs: 22g

9. Banana Muffin

Preparation time: 5 minutes
Cooking time: 20 minutes
Servings: 8
Ingredients:

- 2 bananas
- 1 ¼ cups of wholemeal flour
- 2 tablespoons of applesauce
- 1 tablespoon of ground chia seeds
- 2 tablespoons of maple syrup
- 2 cups of coconut milk
- 2 tablespoons of coconut butter
- half a sachet of organic baking powder
- 1 pinch of salt

Directions:

1. Soak the ground chia seeds with 3 tablespoons of water.
2. In a bowl, mix the apple sauce, the soaked chia seeds, the salt, the milk and the butter.
3. Combine the sifted flour and baking powder, and mix again.

4. Blend the bananas in a mixer and incorporate them into the mixture.
5. Fill the muffin tins to three-quarters of their capacity and bake in a hot oven at 350° F for about 15-20 minutes.

Per serving: Calories: 116kcal; Fat: 4g; Protein: 2g; Carbs: 18g

10. Mushroom Frittata

Preparation time: 15 minutes
Cooking time: 20 minutes
Servings: 6
Ingredients:

- 1½ cups chickpea flour
- 1½ cups water
- 1 teaspoon salt
- 2 tablespoons extra-virgin olive oil
- 1 small red onion, diced
- 2 pints of sliced mushrooms
- 1 teaspoon ground turmeric
- ½ teaspoon ground cumin
- 1 teaspoon salt
- ½ teaspoon black pepper
- 2 tablespoons fresh parsley, chopped

Directions:

1. At 350 degrees F, preheat your oven.
2. In a suitable bowl, slowly whisk the water into the chickpea flour; add the salt and set aside.
3. Add olive oil to a suitable cast-iron or oven-safe skillet over high heat. When the oil is hot, add the onion. Sauté the onion for 3 to 5 minutes or until the onion is softened and slightly translucent.
4. Add the mushrooms and sauté for 5 minutes more. Add the turmeric, cumin, salt, and pepper, and sauté for 1 minute.
5. Pour the batter over the vegetables and sprinkle with the parsley.

6. Place the prepared skillet in the preheated oven and bake for 20 to 25 minutes.
7. Serve warm or at room temperature.

Per serving: Calories: 240kcal; Fat: 7.9g; Protein: 11.4g; Carbs: 33.5g

11. Spicy Quinoa

Preparation time: 10 minutes
Cooking time: 20 minutes
Servings: 4
Ingredients:

- 1 cup quinoa, rinsed
- 2 cups water
- ½ cup shredded coconut
- ¼ cup hemp seeds
- 2 tablespoons flaxseed
- 1 teaspoon ground cinnamon
- 1 teaspoon vanilla extract
- 1 pinch salt
- 1 cup fresh berries of your choice
- ¼ cup chopped hazelnuts

Directions:

1. In a suitable saucepan over high heat, combine the quinoa and water.
2. Bring to a boil, reduce its heat to a simmer, and cook for 15 to 20 minutes until the quinoa is cooked.
3. Stir in the coconut, hemp seeds, flaxseed, cinnamon, vanilla, and salt.
4. Divide the cooked quinoa among four bowls and top each serving with ¼ cup of berries and 1 tablespoon of hazelnuts.

Per serving: Calories: 264kcal; Fat: 10g; Protein: 8g; Carbs: 35.4g

12. Tofu Scramble

Preparation time: 10 minutes
Cooking time: 8 minutes
Servings: 4
Ingredients:

- 3 tablespoons extra-virgin olive oil
- 3 green onions, sliced
- 3 garlic cloves, peeled and sliced
- 1 15-oz package of firm tofu, drained and diced
- Kosher salt, to taste
- 1 cup mung bean sprouts
- 2 tablespoons mint, chopped
- 2 tablespoons parsley, chopped
- 1 tablespoon lime juice
- Fish sauce for serving
- Cooked brown rice for serving

Directions:

1. Mix olive oil, white parts of the green onions, and garlic in the cold sauté pan. Turn the heat to low. As the aromatics warm, occasionally stir for almost 4 minutes.
2. Add the tofu and salt and reduce its heat to medium. Cook, occasionally stirring, until the tofu is well coated with the oil and warmed for 3 minutes.
3. Add mung bean sprouts and cook for 1 minute.
4. Stir in the green parts of the green onions and the mint, parsley, and lime juice.
5. Stir to combine. Taste, adding fish sauce or additional lime juice, if desired.
6. Serve the scramble on its own or with poached eggs on brown rice.

Per serving: Calories: 185kcal; Fat: 14.9g; Protein: 11.1g; Carbs: 5.6g

13. Coconut Pancakes

Preparation time: 10 minutes
Cooking time: 20 minutes
Servings: 4
Ingredients:

- 4 eggs
- 1 cup coconut milk
- 1 tablespoon melted coconut oil
- 1 tablespoon maple syrup
- 1 teaspoon vanilla extract
- ½ cup coconut flour
- 1 teaspoon baking soda
- ½ teaspoon salt

Directions:

1. Mix the eggs, coconut milk, coconut oil, maple syrup, and vanilla in a suitable bowl with an electric mixer.
2. In a suitable bowl, stir together the coconut flour, baking soda, and salt. Add these dry ingredients to the wet ingredients and beat well until smooth and lump-free.
3. Lightly grease a suitable skillet with coconut oil. Place it over medium-high heat.
4. Add the batter in ½-cup scoops and cook for almost 3 minutes, or until golden brown on the bottom. Flip and cook for nearly 2 more minutes.
5. Stack the pancakes on a plate while continuing to cook the remaining batter. This makes about 8 pancakes.

Per serving: Calories: 180kcal; Fat: 10.3g; Protein: 7.8g; Carbs: 14.6g

14. Banana Oatmeal

Preparation time: 5 minutes.
Cooking time: 7 minutes.
Servings: 6
Ingredients:

- 3 cups old-fashioned rolled oats
- ¼ teaspoon salt
- 2 large bananas, mashed (1 heaping cup)
- 2 large eggs, lightly beaten
- ⅓ cup xylitol

Directions:

1. Set the oats, salt, bananas, eggs, and xylitol in a suitable bowl and stir to combine well.
2. Lightly Layer a 6" cake pan with cooking spray. Transfer the oat mixture to this pan.
3. Pour 1½ cups of water into the inner pot. Place a steam rack in the insert of the Instant pot and place this pan on the steam rack. Close the lid and secure it well.
4. Pressure cook for 7 minutes.
5. When done, release the pressure quickly until the float valve drops and then unlock the lid.
6. Allow the oatmeal to cool for 5 minutes before serving.

Per serving: Calories: 139kcal; Fat: 3.1g; Protein: 5.2g; Carbs: 24g

15. Banana Date Porridge

Preparation time: 5 minutes.
Cooking time: 4 minutes.
Servings: 4
Ingredients:

- 1 cup buckwheat groats
- 1½ cups vanilla almond milk, unsweetened
- 1 cup water
- 1 large banana, mashed
- 5 pitted dates, chopped
- ¾ teaspoon ground cinnamon
- ¾ teaspoon pure vanilla extract

Directions:

1. Set the buckwheat groats, almond milk, water, banana, dates, cinnamon, and vanilla in the insert of the Instant pot and stir. Close the lid and secure it well.

2. Pressure cook for 4 minutes.

3. When done, release the pressure quickly until the float valve drops and then unlock the lid.

4. Allow the porridge to cool slightly before spooning it into bowls to serve.

Per serving: Calories: 178kcal; Fat: 2.2g; Protein: 4.8g; Carbs: 37.9g

CHAPTER 2: Vegetables and Sides

16. Sweet Potatoes In Sweet And Sour Sauce

Preparation time: 5 minutes
Cooking time: 20 minutes
Servings: 3
Ingredients:

- 2 tablespoons of coconut oil
- 3 sweet potatoes
- 1 clove of garlic
- 1 chili
- 1 white onion
- 1 tablespoon of cilantro
- 1 pinch of salt
- 3 tablespoons of low sodium soy sauce
- 3 tablespoons of red wine vinegar
- 1 teaspoon of coconut sugar or 1 tablespoon of yacon syrup
- 1 tablespoon of rice flour

Directions:

1. Mix the yacon syrup, soy sauce, vinegar, and rice flour well in a bowl.
2. In a non-stick pan, lightly heat a tablespoon of coconut oil and brown the peeled and diced potatoes for 5 minutes. Add a couple of tablespoons of boiling water and continue cooking until soft. Set them aside.
3. Put the other spoonful of coconut oil in another pan and fry the chopped onion and garlic for 5 minutes. Add the potatoes, mix and add the sauce.
4. Cook for a couple of minutes over moderate heat.
5. Mix with the chopped cilantro and chili. Serve hot.

Per serving: Calories: 156kcal; Fat: 3g; Protein: 3g; Carbs: 30g

17. Salt Cake With Asparagus And Mushroom Cream

Preparation time: 20 minutes
Cooking time: 40 minutes
Servings: 8
Ingredients:

- 2 cups of asparagus
- 4 cups of cremini mushrooms
- 1 tablespoon of Italian seasoning
- 1 tablespoon of olive oil
- 1 tablespoon of coconut butter
- 1 1/2 cups of buckwheat flour
- ¾ cups of rice flour
- 4 tablespoons of sesame oil

Directions:

1. Clean the asparagus and boil them in lightly salted water for 10 minutes, then drain and cut them into small pieces.
2. Put the coconut butter in a non-stick pan and brown the asparagus for 5 minutes. Add salt and pepper.
3. In another pan, put the mushrooms with the olive oil and the Italian seasoning and cook them for about 15 minutes; if necessary, complete the cooking by adding a few tablespoons of warm water.
4. In a bowl, combine a pinch of salt, buckwheat flour and rice flour and mix well.
5. Add the sesame oil and 1/2 cup of slightly warm water and knead.
6. If necessary, add more water, a little at a time.

7. Roll out the dough with a rolling pin and transfer it to an ovenproof dish lined with baking paper.

8. Blend the mushrooms in a blender, spread the cream obtained over the dough, and bake in a hot oven at 350° F for about 30 minutes.

9. Remove the dish from the oven, add the asparagus and bake again for 5 minutes.

Per serving: Calories: 206kcal; Fat: 7g; Protein: 7g; Carbs: 32g

18. Zucchini Fritters With Garlic Sauce

Preparation time: 30 minutes
Cooking time: 15 minutes
Servings: 4
Ingredients:

- 5 courgettes
- 2 organic eggs
- 3 tablespoons of rice flour
- 2 tablespoons of nutritional yeast
- 1 cup unsweetened coconut yogurt
- 3 tablespoons of grated quinoa bread (see recipe)
- 8 fresh mint leaves
- 2 cloves of garlic
- 3 tablespoons of olive oil
- 1 pinch of black pepper
- 1 pinch of salt

Directions:

1. Put the yogurt in a colander with a bowl and put it in the refrigerator for 30 minutes.

2. After this time, the yogurt will have eliminated the excess water; season it with a pinch of salt and minced garlic and put it back in the refrigerator.

3. Wash the courgettes and cut them into julienne strips. Beat the eggs and add them to the courgettes, breadcrumbs,

nutritional yeast, salt and pepper and chopped mint.

4. In a non-stick pan, lightly heat the olive oil and cook the pancakes by spoonfuls, turning them brown on both sides. Serve the fritters hot with the coconut sauce.

Per serving: Calories: 238kcal; Fat: 16g; Protein: 7g; Carbs: 13g

19. Spinach With Leek And Hazelnuts

Preparation time: 10 minutes
Cooking time: 15 minutes
Servings: 2
Ingredients:

- 2 tablespoons of coconut oil
- 2 leeks
- 10 hazelnuts
- 1 clove of garlic
- 1 pinch of nutmeg
- 1 tablespoon of wine vinegar
- 2 cups of spinach
- 1 pinch of salt
- 1 pinch of cayenne pepper

Directions:

1. Chop the garlic and brown it lightly in a non-stick pan with coconut oil. Add the sliced leeks and cook over moderate heat until soft.

2. Add the hazelnuts, vinegar and a pinch of nutmeg.

3. In a saucepan, bring plenty of lightly salted water to a boil and cook the spinach for 15 minutes, drain very well and add to the leeks, mix. Serve hot.

Per serving: Calories: 105kcal; Fat: 9g; Protein: 3g; Carbs: 6g

20. Greek Feta With Tomatoes And Almond Pesto

Preparation time: 5 minutes
Cooking time: 0 minutes
Servings: 3
Ingredients:

- 1 ½ cups of feta
- 1 tablespoon of nutritional yeast
- 4 tablespoons of chopped basil
- 10 almonds
- 1 clove of garlic
- 3 tablespoons of olive oil
- 10 cherry tomatoes
- 5 pitted black olives

Directions:

1. Put the basil, the almonds, a pinch of salt, the nutritional yeast and 2 tablespoons of olive oil in a blender.
2. Blend until creamy.
3. Cut the feta cheese into cubes, add the pesto, the cherry tomatoes cut in half and the olives, mix well and serve.

Per serving: Calories: 341kcal; Fat: 31g; Protein: 12g; Carbs: 7g

21. Artichokes And Beet Frittata

Preparation time: 5 minutes
Cooking time: 10 minutes
Servings: 7
Ingredients:

- 8 organic eggs
- 1 cup of artichoke hearts in oil
- 1 beetroot
- 1 tablespoon of cilantro
- 2 tablespoons of olive oil
- 1 pinch of salt
- 1 pinch of cayenne pepper

Directions:

1. Boil the beetroot in boiling water until soft, drain and cut into cubes.
2. Put the artichokes in a colander and drain the oil well.
3. Beat the eggs, and add the salt, pepper, coriander, artichokes and beetroot.
4. Grease a non-stick pan with olive oil, heat slightly, and pour in the preparation.
5. Cook for 5 minutes on each side.

Per serving: Calories: 141kcal; Fat: 4g; Protein: 8g; Carbs: 4g

22. Potato Croquettes With Pumpkin Seeds

Preparation time: 5 minutes + 20 of rest
Cooking time: 15 minutes
Servings: 6
Ingredients:

- 3 cups of rice flour
- 1 teaspoon of dried sage
- 1 organic egg
- 3 cups unsweetened almond milk
- olive oil for frying
- 3 yellow potatoes
- 1 ½ cups of ricotta cheese
- 2 tablespoons of pumpkin seeds
- 1 pinch of salt
- 1 pinch of black pepper

Directions:

1. Mix the flour with the sage and a pinch of salt.
2. Beat the eggs with the milk, add them to the flour and mix. Let it rest in the refrigerator for 20 minutes.
3. Heat a tablespoon of oil in a non-stick pan and brown the potatoes made in small cubes for 5 minutes.

4. Add a few tablespoons of boiling water and cook until they become soft. Transfer them to a bowl.

5. Mix well with the ricotta, the pumpkin seeds, and the egg and milk batter.

6. Heat the olive oil in a pan and cook the mixture in spoonfuls for 3 minutes, then turn over to the other side and cook another 3 minutes. Serve hot.

Per serving: Calories: 236kcal; Fat: 6g; Protein: 9g; Carbs: 37g

23. Tempeh With Olives And Capers

Preparation time: 5 minutes
Cooking time: 8 minutes
Servings: 3
Ingredients:

- 4 ¾ cups of tempeh
- 2 tablespoons of black olives
- 2 chopped shallots
- 2 teaspoons of paprika
- 2 tablespoons of olive oil
- 1 pinch of salt
- 1 pinch of cayenne pepper

Directions:

1. In a non-stick pan, lightly heat the olive oil and brown the shallots for 5 minutes.

2. Add the diced tempeh, paprika and chopped olives.

3. Add the salt and pepper and cook for 3 minutes, stirring.

Per serving: Calories: 317kcal; Fat: 18g; Protein: 29g; Carbs: 43g

24. Rolls Of Quinoa Lettuce And Raspberries

Preparation time: 15 minutes
Cooking time: 15 minutes
Servings: 3
Ingredients:

- 1 ½ cups of quinoa
- 1 head of lettuce
- 1 cucumber
- 10 cherry tomatoes
- 1 tablespoon of chopped fresh mint leaves
- 2 tablespoons of raspberries
- 1 organic lemon
- 3 tablespoons of olive oil
- 3 tablespoons of cottage cheese
- 1 pinch of salt
- 1 pinch of cayenne pepper

Directions:

1. Cook the quinoa in plenty of lightly salted water for about 15 minutes, and drain well.

2. Remove the larger leaves from the lettuce without breaking them, and wash them.

3. Peel the cucumber and cut it into thin slices.

4. Wash the cherry tomatoes and cut them into four parts.

5. Put the raspberries in a blender with the mint, lemon juice and olive oil and blend well.

6. Mix the quinoa with the cucumber, cherry tomatoes, cheese and raspberry sauce.

7. Spread the quinoa filling in the center of the salad leaves and close with a toothpick.

Per serving: Calories: 310kcal; Fat: 14g; Protein: 10g; Carbs: 39g

25. Millet Meatballs With Broccoli

Preparation time: 10 minutes
Cooking time: 25 minutes
Servings: 5
Ingredients:

- 2 cups of boiled broccoli
- 1 ½ cups of millet
- 1 yellow potato
- 4 tablespoons of grated quinoa bread (see recipe)
- 2 tablespoons of olive oil
- 1 pinch of salt
- 1 pinch of pepper
- sunflower oil for frying

Directions:

1. Peel and boil the potato, drain it and add it to the broccoli.
2. In a bowl, mash the potato and broccoli with a fork and add salt, pepper, and a tablespoon of olive oil.
3. Coarsely chop the slices of quinoa bread in a blender.
4. Heat the frying oil in a pan; in the meantime, form balls with your hands with the broccoli and potato mixture and pass them in the breadcrumbs.
5. Dip the meatballs in the oil and fry until golden.
6. Remove excess oil by placing the meatballs on paper towels. Serve hot.

Per serving: Calories: 245kcal; Fat: 6g; Protein: 8g; Carbs: 27g

26. Piadine Of Chickpeas With Spinach And Mayonnaise

Preparation time: 20 minutes
Cooking time: 25 minutes
Servings: 8
Ingredients:

- 1/2 cup of coconut milk
- 3/4 cup sunflower oil
- 1 tablespoon of mustard
- the juice of half a lemon
- 1 teaspoon of vinegar
- 1 cup of spinach

- 2 cups of chickpea flour
- 1 pinch of salt
- 1 pinch of black pepper
- 4 tablespoons of olive oil

Directions:

1. Put the sunflower oil in a mixer with the coconut milk, mustard, vinegar, and lemon and blend at maximum speed for 1 minute; add the vinegar and blend for a minute more.
2. Put the prepared mayonnaise in the refrigerator.
3. Put the chickpea flour in a bowl and slowly mix in the water until the dough is smooth and thick. Add a tablespoon of olive oil and a pinch of salt and mix.
4. Put in the refrigerator to rest.
5. Meanwhile, sauté the spinach in a non-stick pan with a pinch of salt and a tablespoon of olive oil.
6. Put the spinach in a bowl in the same pan. After greasing the remaining oil with a kitchen brush, cook the wraps with a spoonful.
7. Pour a ladle of batter, wait for it to distribute in the pan, dry, and turn it to the other side. Continue until the batter is finished.
8. Fill the chickpeas wraps with spinach and mayonnaise.

Per serving: Calories: 269kcal; Fat: 14g; Protein: 10g; Carbs: 23g

27. Caramelized Rape With Hazelnuts

Preparation time: 15 minutes
Cooking time: 20 minutes
Servings: 3
Ingredients:

- 2 cups of boiled turnips
- 7 tablespoons of fig jam
- 2 tablespoons of red wine vinegar

- 40 black grapes
- 1/3 cup of hazelnuts
- 1 cup unsweetened soy yogurt
- 2 tablespoons of fresh basil
- 1 pinch of cayenne pepper
- 1 pinch of salt

Directions:

1. Mix the fig jam with balsamic vinegar in a saucepan over meager heat. When it has melted, add the boiled turnips and allow them to flavor. Add the grapes and cook for another 10 minutes.
2. Add the hazelnuts, salt, pepper, basil and yogurt.
3. Serve hot.

Per serving: Calories: 278kcal; Fat: 10g; Protein: 4g; Carbs: 43g

28. Roasted Broccoli and Cashews

Preparation time: 10 minutes
Cooking time: 20 minutes
Servings: 4
Ingredients:

- 6 cups broccoli florets
- 2 tablespoons extra-virgin olive oil
- 1 teaspoon salt
- 1 tablespoon coconut aminos
- ½ cup toasted cashews

Directions:

1. At 375 degrees F, preheat your oven.
2. In a suitable bowl, toss the broccoli with olive oil and salt.
3. Transfer the prepared broccoli to a baking sheet into a single layer.
4. Place the broccoli sheet in the preheated oven and roast for 15 to 20 minutes or until the broccoli is tender.

5. In a suitable bowl, toss the roasted broccoli with the coconut aminos and cashews, and serve.

Per serving: Calories: 108kcal; Fat: 7.5g; Protein: 3.8g; Carbs: 9.3g

29. Ginger Sweet Potatoes and Pea Hash

Preparation time: 10 minutes
Cooking time: 10 minutes
Servings: 4
Ingredients:

- 2 tablespoons coconut oil
- 4 scallions, sliced
- 3 garlic cloves, minced
- 2 teaspoons minced fresh ginger
- 1 teaspoon curry powder
- 1 teaspoon salt
- ½ teaspoon ground turmeric
- 2 sweet potatoes, roasted, peeled and chopped
- 1 cup frozen peas
- 2 cups cooked brown rice
- 1 tablespoon coconut aminos
- ¼ cup chopped fresh cilantro
- ½ cup chopped cashews

Directions:

1. In a suitable skillet over medium-high heat, melt the coconut oil. Add the scallions, garlic, ginger, curry powder, salt, and turmeric. Sauté for 2 minutes, or until fragrant.
2. Stir in the sweet potatoes, peas, brown rice, and coconut aminos. Sauté for 5 minutes.
3. Transfer the hash to a serving dish and garnish with the cilantro and cashews.

Per serving: Calories: 424kcal; Fat: 11.8g; Protein: 9g; Carbs: 71.9g

30. Buckwheat and Sweet Potatoes

Preparation time: 15 minutes
Cooking time: 20 minutes
Servings: 4 to 6
Ingredients:

- 1 tablespoon coconut oil
- 2 cups cubed sweet potatoes
- 1 yellow onion, chopped
- 2 garlic cloves, minced
- 2 teaspoons ground cumin
- ½ cup buckwheat groats
- 1 cup lentils, rinsed
- 6 cups vegetable broth
- 1 teaspoon salt
- ½ teaspoon black pepper
- 2 cups chopped kale, washed and stemmed

Directions:

1. In a suitable pot over medium-high heat, melt the coconut oil. Stir in the sweet potatoes, onion, garlic, and cumin. Sauté for 5 minutes.
2. Add the buckwheat groats, lentils, vegetable broth, salt, and pepper. Bring to a boil. Reduce its heat to simmer, and cover the pot. Cook for 15 minutes until the sweet potatoes, buckwheat, and lentils are tender.
3. Remove the pot from the heat. Add the kale and stir to combine.
4. Cover this cooking pot and let it sit for 5 minutes before serving.

Per serving: Calories: 406kcal; Fat: 6.7g; Protein: 24.2g; Carbs: 64.5g

CHAPTER 3: Beans and Grains

31. Curry Pastinache Cream With Leek And Black Beans

Preparation time: 10 minutes
Cooking time: 30 minutes
Servings: 4
Ingredients:

- 4 cups of parsnips
- 3 cups low sodium vegetable broth
- 2 leeks
- 1 ½ cups of boiled black beans
- 2 tablespoons of olive oil
- 1 teaspoon of Italian seasoning
- 1 teaspoon of saffron powder
- 1 pinch of cayenne pepper
- 1 pinch of salt

Directions:

1. Peel the pastiche and make them into cubes.
2. Brown them for 5 minutes in a non-stick pan with the olive oil, add the vegetable broth, saffron, and Italian seasoning and cook for about 25 minutes.
3. Wash the leek and cut it into slices.
4. Brown it in a non-stick pan with a tablespoon of olive oil for 3 minutes, add the beans, let them flavor and transfer to a bowl.
5. Place the parsnips in a blender and blend until creamy. Combine with the black beans and leeks and serve hot.

Per serving: Calories: 219kcal; Fat: 7g; Protein: 8g; Carbs: 36g

32. Basic Beans

Preparation time: 30 minutes

Cooking time: 7 to 8 hours
Servings: 6 cups
Ingredients:

- 1 pound (454 g) of dried beans, soaked for at least 8 hours
- Water

Directions:

1. Drain and rinse the beans well. Put them in the slow cooker and cover them with 2 inches of fresh water.
2. Cover and cook on low for 7 to 8 hours, or until soft and cooked.
3. Drain and serve

Per serving: Calories: 259kcal; Fat: 0g; Protein: 15g; Carbs: 48g

33. Coconut Brown Rice

Preparation time: 15 minutes
Cooking time: 3 hours
Servings: 4 to 6
Ingredients:

- 2 cups brown rice, soaked in water overnight, drained and rinsed
- 3 cups water
- 1½ cups full-fat coconut milk
- 1 teaspoon sea salt
- ½ teaspoon ground ginger
- Freshly ground black pepper, to taste

Directions:

1. In a slow cooker, combine all the ingredients and stir to combine.
2. Cover and cook on high for 3 hours and serve.

Per serving: Calories: 479kcal; Fat: 19g; Protein: 9g; Carbs: 73g

34. Herbed Harvest Rice

Preparation time: 15 minutes
Cooking time: 3 hours
Servings: 4 to 6
Ingredients:

- 2 cups brown rice, soaked in water overnight, drained and rinsed
- ½ small onion, chopped
- 4 cups vegetable broth
- 2 tablespoons extra-virgin olive oil
- ½ teaspoon dried thyme leaves
- ½ teaspoon garlic powder
- ½ cup cooked sliced mushrooms
- ½ cup dried cranberries
- ½ cup toasted pecans

Directions:

1. In a slow cooker, combine the rice, onion, broth, olive oil, thyme, and garlic powder. Stir well.
2. Cover and cook on high for 3 hours.
3. Stir in the mushrooms, cranberries, and pecans, and serve.

Per serving: Calories: 258kcal; Fat: 12g; Protein: 6g; Carbs: 38g

35. Spanish Rice

Preparation time: 15 minutes
Cooking time: 5 to 6 hours
Servings: 4 to 6
Ingredients:

- 2 cups white rice
- 2 cups vegetable broth
- 2 tablespoons extra-virgin olive oil
- 1 (14½-ounce 411-g) can of crushed tomatoes
- 1 (4-ounce 113-g) can Hatch green chiles
- ½ medium onion, diced
- 1 teaspoon sea salt
- ½ teaspoon ground cumin
- ½ teaspoon garlic powder
- ½ teaspoon chili powder
- ½ teaspoon dried oregano
- Freshly ground black pepper, to taste

Directions:

1. In a slow cooker, combine all the ingredients and stir.
2. Cover and cook on low for 5 to 6 hours, fluff, and serve.

Per serving: Calories: 406kcal; Fat: 7g; Protein: 8g; Carbs: 79g

36. Brown Rice with Bell Peppers

Preparation time: 10 minutes
Cooking time: 10 minutes
Servings: 4
Ingredients:

- 2 tablespoons extra-virgin olive oil
- 1 red bell pepper, chopped
- 1 green bell pepper, chopped
- 1 onion, chopped
- 2 cups cooked brown rice
- 2 tablespoons low-sodium soy sauce

Directions:

1. Heat the olive oil in a large nonstick skillet over medium-high heat until it shimmers.
2. Add bell peppers and onion. Cook for about 7 minutes, until brown.
3. Add the rice and the soy sauce. Cook for about 3 minutes, until the rice warms through.

Per serving: Calories: 266kcal; Fat: 8g; Protein: 5g; Carbs: 44g

37. Bean and Rice Casserole

Preparation time: 10 minutes
Cooking time: 35 minutes
Servings: 4
Ingredients:

- 1 cup soaked black beans
- 2 cups water
- 2 teaspoons onion powder
- 2 teaspoons chili powder, optional
- 2 cups brown rice
- 6 ounces (170 g) tomato paste
- 1 teaspoon minced garlic
- 1 teaspoon sea salt

Directions:

1. Combine all of the ingredients in your Instant Pot. Choose the "Manual" setting and seal the lid.
2. Cook for 35 minutes under high pressure.
3. Once the cooking is complete, let the pressure release for 5 minutes.
4. Then perform a quick pressure release. Serve hot.

Per serving: Calories: 444kcal; Fat: 4g; Protein: 20g; Carbs: 82g

38. Herby Quinoa with Walnuts

Preparation time: 20 minutes
Cooking time: 10 to 15 minutes
Servings: 4
Ingredients:

- 2 minced sun-dried tomatoes
- 1 cup quinoa
- 2 cups vegetable broth
- 2 garlic cloves, minced
- ¼ cup chopped chives
- 2 tablespoons chopped parsley
- 2 tablespoons chopped basil
- 2 tablespoons chopped mint
- 1 tablespoon olive oil
- ½ teaspoon lemon zest
- 1 tablespoon lemon juice
- 2 tablespoons minced walnuts

Directions:

1. In a pot, combine quinoa, vegetable broth, and garlic.
2. Boil until the quinoa is tender and the liquid absorbs for 10 to 15 minutes.
3. Stir in chives, parsley, basil, mint, tomatoes, olive oil, zest, lemon juice, and walnuts.
4. Warm for 5 minutes. Serve.

Per serving: Calories: 308kcal; Fat: 8g; Protein: 28g; Carbs: 31g

39. Chipotle Kidney Bean Chili

Preparation time: 20 minutes
Cooking time: 25 minutes
Servings: 4
Ingredients:

- 2 tablespoons olive oil
- 1 onion, chopped
- 2 garlic cloves, minced
- 1 (16-ounce 454-g) can tomato sauce
- 1 tablespoon chili powder
- 1 chipotle chili, minced
- 1 teaspoon ground cumin
- ½ teaspoon dried marjoram
- 1 (15½-ounce 439-g) can of kidney beans
- Sea salt and pepper to taste
- ½ teaspoon cayenne pepper

Directions:

1. Heat the oil in a pot over medium heat.
2. Place in onion and garlic and sauté for 3 minutes.
3. Put in tomato sauce, chipotle chili, chili powder, cumin, cayenne pepper,

marjoram, salt, and pepper and cook for 5 minutes.

4. Stir in kidney beans and 2 cups of water.
5. Bring to a boil, lower the heat and simmer for 15 minutes, stirring often.

Per serving: Calories: 271kcal; Fat: 11g; Protein: 6g; Carbs: 37g

40. Southern Bean Bowl

Preparation time: 15 minutes
Cooking time: 0 minutes
Servings: 4
Ingredients:

- 1 tomato, chopped
- 1 red bell pepper, chopped
- 1 green bell pepper, chopped
- 1 small red onion, sliced
- 1 (14½-ounce 411-g) can of black-eyed peas
- 1 (14½-ounce 411-g) can of black beans
- ¼ cup capers
- 2 avocados pitted
- 1 tablespoon lemon juice
- ¼ cup sake
- 1 teaspoon dried oregano
- Sea salt to taste
- 2 tablespoons olive oil
- 1 cup leafy greens, chopped

Directions:

1. Mix the tomato, peppers, onion, black-eyed peas, beans, and capers in a bowl.
2. Put the avocados, lemon juice, sake, olive oil, oregano, and salt in a food processor and blitz until smooth.
3. Add the dressing to the bean bowl and toss to combine.
4. Top with leafy greens to serve.

Per serving: Calories: 412kcal; Fat: 21g; Protein: 7g; Carbs: 48g

41. Indian Butter Chickpeas

Preparation time: 15 minutes
Cooking time: 6 to 8 hours
Servings: 4 to 6
Ingredients:

- 1 tablespoon coconut oil
- 1 medium onion, diced
- 1 pound (454 g) dried chickpeas, soaked in water overnight, drained, and rinsed
- 2 cups full-fat coconut milk
- 1 (14½-ounce 411-g) can of crushed tomatoes
- 2 tablespoons almond butter
- 2 tablespoons curry powder
- 1½ teaspoons garlic powder
- 1 teaspoon ground ginger
- ½ teaspoon sea salt
- ½ teaspoon ground cumin
- ½ teaspoon chili powder

Directions:

1. Coat the slow cooker with coconut oil.
2. Layer the onion along the bottom of the slow cooker.
3. Add the remaining ingredients and stir to combine.
4. Cover and cook on low for 6 to 8 hours, until the chickpeas are soft, and serve.

Per serving: Calories: 720kcal; Fat: 30g; Protein: 27g; Carbs: 86g

42. Mushroom Risotto with Spring Peas

Preparation time: 15 minutes
Cooking time: 2 to 3 hours
Servings: 4 to 6
Ingredients:

- 1½ cups Arborio rice
- 1 cup of English peas
- 1 small shallot, minced

- ¼ cup dried porcini mushrooms
- 4½ cups broth of choice (choose a vegetable to keep it vegan)
- 1 tablespoon freshly squeezed lemon juice
- ½ teaspoon garlic powder
- ½ teaspoon sea salt

Directions:

1. In a slow cooker, combine all the ingredients and stir to mix well.
2. Cover and cook on high for 2 to 3 hours and serve.

Per serving: Calories: 382kcal; Fat: 1g; Protein: 12g; Carbs: 79g

43. Grandma's Black Bean Chili

Preparation time: 15 minutes
Cooking time: 20 minutes
Servings: 4
Ingredients:

- 2 tablespoons olive oil
- 1 teaspoon smoked paprika
- 1 onion, chopped
- 2 (28-ounce 794-g) cans of diced tomatoes
- 2 (14-ounce 397-g) cans of black beans
- 1 chili pepper, chopped
- 1 teaspoon garlic powder
- ½ teaspoon sea salt

Directions:

1. Warm the olive oil in a pot over medium heat, place the onion, and cook for 5 minutes until tender.
2. Mix in tomatoes, black beans, chili pepper, garlic powder, smoked paprika, and salt and bring to a simmer.
3. Then low the heat and cook for 15 more minutes.
4. Serve warm.

Per serving: Calories: 338kcal; Fat: 9g; Protein: 17g; Carbs: 54g

44. Bean and Spinach Casserole

Preparation time: 20 minutes
Cooking time: 30 minutes
Servings: 6
Ingredients:

- ½ cup whole-wheat bread crumbs
- 1 (15½-ounce 439-g) can of Great Northern beans
- 1 (15½-ounce 439-g) can Navy beans
- 3 tablespoons olive oil
- 1 onion, chopped
- 2 carrots, chopped
- 1 celery stalk, chopped
- 2 garlic cloves, minced
- 1 cup baby spinach
- 3 tomatoes, chopped
- 1 cup vegetable broth
- 1 tablespoon parsley, chopped
- 1 teaspoon dried thyme
- Sea salt and pepper to taste

Directions:

1. Preheat your oven to 380°F (193°C). Heat the oil in a skillet over medium heat.
2. Place in onion, carrots, celery, and garlic. Sauté for 5 minutes. Remove into a greased casserole.
3. Add beans, spinach, tomatoes, broth, parsley, thyme, salt, and pepper and stir to combine.
4. Cover with foil and bake in the oven for 15 minutes.
5. Take the casserole from the oven, remove the foil, and spread the bread crumbs.
6. Bake for another 10 minutes until the top is crispy and golden.

7. Serve warm.

Per serving: Calories: 332kcal; Fat: 8g; Protein: 16g; Carbs: 49g

45. Mediterranean Quinoa with Peperoncini

Preparation time: 15 minutes
Cooking time: 6 to 8 hours
Servings: 4 to 6
Ingredients:

- 1½ cups quinoa rinsed well
- 3 cups vegetable broth
- ½ teaspoon sea salt
- ½ teaspoon garlic powder
- ¼ teaspoon dried oregano
- ¼ teaspoon dried basil leaves
- Freshly ground black pepper, to taste
- 3 cups arugula
- ½ cup diced tomatoes
- ⅓ cup sliced peperoncini
- ¼ cup freshly squeezed lemon juice
- 3 tablespoons extra-virgin olive oil

Directions:

1. In a slow cooker, combine the first seven ingredients.
2. Cover and cook on low for 6 to 8 hours.
3. In a large bowl, toss together the remaining ingredients.
4. When the quinoa is done, add it to the arugula salad, mix well, and serve.

Per serving: Calories: 359kcal; Fat: 14g; Protein: 10g; Carbs: 50g

CHAPTER 4: Fish and Seafood

46. Salmon With Rocket Pesto

Preparation time: 10 minutes
Cooking time: 10 minutes
Servings: 4
Ingredients:

- 4 wild salmon fillets
- 2 tablespoons of parsley
- 1 cup of rocket
- 2 cloves of garlic
- 1 organic lemon
- 3 tablespoons of olive oil
- 5 tablespoons of cashews
- 1 pinch of salt
- 1 pinch of cayenne pepper

Directions:

1. Wash and put the rocket, garlic, cashews, a pinch of salt and a tablespoon of oil in a mixer and blend well.
2. Put the pesto obtained in the refrigerator.
3. Wash the salmon, brush it with oil and place it on a baking sheet covered with parchment paper at 400° F for about 10 minutes.
4. Remove the salmon from the oven and cover it with the pesto.

Per serving: Calories: 346kcal; Fat: 27g; Protein: 18g; Carbs: 7g

47. Cabbage With Anchovies

Preparation time: 10 minutes
Cooking time: 0 minutes
Servings: 2
Ingredients:

- 2 cups of boiled cabbage
- 2 tablespoons of capers
- 5 anchovies in oil
- 2 tomatoes
- 1 chili
- 2 tablespoons of olive oil
- 1 pinch of salt
- 1 pinch of cayenne pepper
- 1 tablespoon of chopped fresh parsley

Directions:

1. Mix the anchovies cut into small pieces in a bowl, the chopped chili pepper, the parsley, the whole capers, the diced tomatoes, the oil, the salt, and the pepper.
2. Add the cabbage and mix again.

Per serving: Calories: 257kcal; Fat: 19g; Protein: 12g; Carbs: 11g

48. Wholemeal Pasta With Sardines And Leeks

Preparation time: 5 minutes
Cooking time: 15 minutes
Servings: 3
Ingredients:

- 8 ounces of wholemeal pasta
- 2 leeks
- 1 basket of radicchio
- 8 clean sardines
- 2 tablespoons of olive oil
- 1 pinch of salt
- 1 pinch of pepper

Directions:

1. Clean and cut the leeks into thin slices.
2. In a non-stick pan, sauté the leeks with the oil, the chopped radicchio, and the sardines cut into small pieces, add the

salt and pepper and cook, stirring, for 10 minutes.

3. In a pot with plenty of lightly salted boiling water, cook the pasta for the cooking time indicated on the package, drain well and season with the prepared sardine sauce.

Per serving: Calories: 237kcal; Fat: 11g; Protein: 13g; Carbs: 22g

49. Salmon Salad With Mushrooms And Broccoli

Preparation time: 5 minutes
Cooking time: 10 minutes
Servings: 2
Ingredients:

- 8 ounces of smoked wild salmon
- ¾ cups of cremini mushrooms
- 1 cup of boiled broccoli
- 2 tablespoons of chopped parsley
- 2 tablespoons of olive oil
- 1 pinch of salt
- 1 pinch of cayenne pepper
- 1 organic lemon

Directions:

1. Cut the salmon into strips and marinate in the lemon juice.
2. Wash the mushrooms, cut them into skinny slices and add them to the salmon.
3. In a non-stick pan, heat the oil and pour the broccoli. Add the salt, pepper, and brown for 5 minutes.
4. Drain the lemon juice from the salmon and mushrooms and put them in a bowl. Add the broccoli and parsley, and serve.

Per serving: Calories: 298kcal; Fat: 19g; Protein: 26g; Carbs: 4g

50. Cod And Pumpkin Fishballs With White Sauce

Preparation time: 10 minutes
Cooking time: 25 minutes
Servings: 4
Ingredients:

- 8 ounces of cod
- 1 cup boiled pumpkin cubes
- 1 cup unsweetened soy yogurt
- 1 tablespoon of mustard
- 5 tablespoons of grated wholemeal bread
- 3 tablespoons of corn flour
- 5 tablespoons of olive oil
- 1 tablespoon of chopped parsley
- 1 pinch of salt
- 1 pinch of pepper

Directions:

1. Put the yogurt, mustard and parsley in the mixer and chop.
2. Set the sauce aside. In a non-stick pan with a tablespoon of oil, cook the cod for 5 minutes and then chop it coarsely.
3. Mash the pumpkin with a fork, add the cod and a tablespoon of oil, a pinch of salt and pepper, and a tablespoon of breadcrumbs.
4. Mix the ingredients well and shape them into balls with your hands.
5. Dip the balls in the cornmeal mixed with the breadcrumbs and place them on a baking sheet lined with parchment paper.
6. Heat the oven to 400° F and bake for 10 minutes. Serve with the sauce.

Per serving: Calories: 233kcal; Fat: 13g; Protein: 16g; Carbs: 3g

51. Mackerel With Sesame And Soy Sprouts

Preparation time: 15 minutes
Cooking time: 10 minutes
Servings: 5
Ingredients:

- 14 ounces of mackerel fillets in oil
- 2 yellow peppers
- 2 cloves of garlic
- 1 ½ cups of red beans
- 1 tablespoon of capers
- 1 cup of bean sprouts
- 1 organic lemon
- 1 tablespoon of sesame seeds
- 2 tablespoons of olive oil
- 1 pinch of salt
- 1 pinch of black pepper

Directions:

1. Chop the garlic. In a non-stick pan, heat a tablespoon of olive oil.
2. Clean the peppers by removing the stalk, cutting them in two and removing the seeds inside.
3. Cut the peppers into strips.
4. Sauté the garlic in the oil for a minute, then add the peppers, capers and pepper and cook until soft.
5. Crumble the mackerel fillets with your hands after draining them from the excess oil and mix with the sesame seeds.
6. In a bowl, combine the mackerel, peppers, and bean sprouts and mix well.

Per serving: Calories: 346kcal; Fat: 22g; Protein: 20g; Carbs: 17g

52. Quinoa With Tuna Pesto

Preparation time: 10 minutes
Cooking time: 20 minutes
Servings: 4
Ingredients:

- 14 ounces of quinoa
- 1 ½ cups of tuna in water
- ¾ cup of feta
- 1 tomato
- 1 cucumber
- 1 tablespoon of hazelnuts
- 1 tablespoon of chopped basil
- 1 pinch of salt
- 1 pinch of cayenne pepper
- 1 tablespoon of olive oil

Directions:

1. Cook the quinoa in plenty of lightly salted boiling water for 15-20 minutes and drain well.
2. Put the tuna in the blender with the feta, hazelnuts, basil and olive oil and blend until smooth.
3. Wash and dice the tomato.
4. Remove the peel from the cucumber and cut it into thin slices.
5. Combine the quinoa with the vegetables and the sauce and mix well.

Per serving: Calories: 262kcal; Fat: 9g; Protein: 22g; Carbs: 25g

53. Soup Of Oysters And Mushrooms

Preparation time: 10 minutes
Cooking time: 50 minutes
Servings: 6
Ingredients:

- 15 oysters
- 1 teaspoon of oregano
- 1 teaspoon of thyme
- 1 cup of white mushrooms

- 2 cups low sodium vegetable broth
- 1 onion
- 1 leek
- 1 yellow potato
- 1 tablespoon of coconut butter

Directions:

1. In a non-stick pan, melt the coconut butter, brown the chopped onion and leek.
2. Add the sliced mushrooms, mix and after a minute, add the vegetable broth and cook for 20 minutes over moderate heat.
3. Add the thyme and oregano.
4. Cut the potato into cubes, add it and cook for another 20 minutes.
5. Wash the oysters well, and put them in a saucepan with the lid on low heat to make them open.
6. Once opened, extract the molluscs and filter the liquid they have released with a strainer.
7. Add the liquid to the mushrooms and potatoes.
8. Cook for another 3 minutes, add the oysters, mix and serve.

Per serving: Calories: 101kcal; Fat: 8g; Protein: 7g; Carbs: 9g

54. Seaweed Fritters Nori And Carrots

Preparation time: 5 minutes
Cooking time: 20 minutes
Servings: 6
Ingredients:

- 3 carrots
- 1 white onion
- 7 tablespoons of rice flour
- 2 tablespoons of sesame oil
- 2 sheets of nori seaweed
- 1 pinch of salt
- sunflower oil for frying

Directions:

1. Grate the carrots and onion; cut the nori seaweed into small squares.
2. Mix the rice flour with the salt, add water until you get a very thick paste, add the vegetables and mix well.
3. In a pan, heat the sunflower oil; when it is boiling, pour the mixture in spoonfuls and cook the pancakes until they are golden on both sides.
4. Season with a pinch of salt and serve hot.

Per serving: Calories: 148kcal; Fat: 4g; Protein: 2g; Carbs: 23g

55. Cod With Creamy Onions

Preparation time: 5 minutes
Cooking time: 35 minutes
Servings: 4
Ingredients:

- 18 ounces of mackerel in oil
- 1 organic lemon
- 2 cloves of garlic
- 4 tablespoons of olive oil
- 6 white onions
- 4 tablespoons of maple syrup
- 2 oranges
- 1 salt lace
- 1 pinch of pepper

Directions:

1. Chop the onions in a non-stick saucepan with 1 tablespoon of olive oil; brown for 5 minutes.
2. Set the heat to low, add 6 tablespoons of water, the orange juice and maple syrup, cook covered for about 20 minutes, and check that the boil is at a minimum and that the onions do not burn.

3. Drain the mackerel from the oil, and put it to marinate in the remaining oil mixed with minced garlic, a pinch of salt, pepper, and lemon juice.

4. Serve the mackerel with creamy onions.

Per serving: Calories: 559kcal; Fat: 32g; Protein: 31g; Carbs: 38g

56. Squid Rings With Saffron

Preparation time: 10 minutes
Cooking time: 15 minutes
Servings: 4
Ingredients:

- 14 ounces of squid rings
- 2 tomatoes
- 1/4 cup low sodium vegetable broth
- 1 red onion
- 1 tablespoon of thyme
- 1 sachet of saffron
- 4 tablespoons of olive oil
- 1 salt lace
- 1 pinch of cayenne pepper

Directions:

1. Wash and cut the tomatoes into cubes.
2. Chop the onion and brown it for 5 minutes in a non-stick pan with a tablespoon of olive oil.
3. Add the squid rings, cook for a minute, add the salt and pepper, add the broth, and cook for another two minutes.
4. In another pan, heat the remaining oil, brown the thyme with the saffron and diced tomatoes, add a pinch of salt and cayenne pepper and cook for about 5 minutes.
5. Pour the tomatoes over the squid and serve hot.

Per serving: Calories: 266kcal; Fat: 16g; Protein: 22g; Carbs: 38g

57. Fish Sticks with Avocado Dipping Sauce

Preparation time: 15 minutes
Cooking time: 5 minutes
Servings: 4
Ingredients:
For the avocado dipping sauce

- 2 avocados
- ¼ cup lime juice
- 2 tablespoons fresh cilantro leaves
- 2 tablespoons olive oil
- 1 teaspoon salt
- 1 teaspoon garlic powder
- Dash ground cumin
- Black pepper

For the fish sticks

- 1½ cups almond flour
- 1 teaspoon salt
- ½ teaspoon paprika
- ¼ teaspoon black pepper
- 3 eggs
- ¼ cup coconut oil
- 1 pound cod fillets, cut into 4-inch-long, 1-inch-thick strips
- Juice of 1 lemon

Directions:

1. In a suitable food processor, blend the avocados, lime juice, cilantro, olive oil, salt, garlic powder, and cumin, and season with pepper until smooth
2. Mix the almond flour, salt, paprika, and pepper in a small shallow bowl. Whisk the eggs in another small shallow bowl.
3. Dip the fish sticks into the egg and the almond flour mixture until fully coated.
4. In a suitable skillet over medium-high heat, heat the coconut oil.
5. One at a time, place the fish sticks in the skillet. Cook for almost 2 minutes on

each side until lightly browned. Apportion them between 2 plates.

6. To serve, sprinkle with the lemon juice and serve alongside the avocado dipping sauce.

Per serving: Calories: 583kcal; Fat: 50g; Protein: 25g; Carbs: 14g

58. Whitefish Curry

Preparation time: 15 minutes
Cooking time: 15 minutes
Servings: 4 to 6
Ingredients:

- 2 tablespoons coconut oil
- 1 onion, chopped
- 2 garlic cloves, minced
- 1 tablespoon minced fresh ginger
- 2 teaspoons curry powder
- 1 teaspoon salt
- ¼ teaspoon black pepper
- 1 (4-inch) piece of lemongrass
- 2 cups cubed butternut squash
- 2 cups chopped broccoli
- 1 (13.5-ounce) can of coconut milk
- 1 cup vegetable broth or chicken broth
- 1 pound firm whitefish fillets
- ¼ cup chopped fresh cilantro
- 1 scallion, sliced thin
- Lemon wedges, for garnish

Directions:

1. In a suitable pot, melt the coconut oil over medium-high heat; add the onion, garlic, ginger, curry powder, salt, and pepper, and sauté them for 5 minutes.

2. Add the lemongrass, butternut squash, broccoli, and sauté them for 2 minutes more.

3. Stir in the coconut milk and vegetable broth and bring to a boil. Reduce its heat to simmer and add the fish. Cover the pot and simmer for 5 minutes until the fish is cooked. Remove and discard the lemongrass.

4. Spoon the curry into a serving bowl. Garnish with the cilantro and scallion, and serve with the lemon wedges.

Per serving: Calories: 553kcal; Fat: 39g; Protein: 34g; Carbs: 22g

59. Coconut-Crusted Shrimp

Preparation time: 10 minutes
Cooking time: 6 minutes
Servings: 4
Ingredients:

- 2 eggs
- 1 cup unsweetened dried coconut
- ¼ cup coconut flour
- ½ teaspoon salt
- ¼ teaspoon paprika
- Dash cayenne pepper
- Dash black pepper
- ¼ cup coconut oil
- 1 pound raw shrimp, peeled and deveined

Directions:

1. In a small shallow bowl, beat all the eggs.

2. Mix the coconut, coconut flour, salt, paprika, cayenne pepper, and black pepper in another small shallow bowl.

3. In a suitable skillet, heat the coconut oil over medium-high heat.

4. Pat the shrimp dry with a paper towel.

5. Working one at a time, hold each shrimp by the tail, dip it into the egg mixture, and then into the coconut mixture until coated. Place into the hot skillet. Cook for almost 3 minutes on each side.

6. Transfer the hot shrimp to a paper towel-lined plate to drain excess oil.

7. Serve immediately.

Per serving: Calories: 279kcal; Fat: 2 0g; Protein: 19g; Carbs: 6g

60. Ahi Poke with Cucumber

Preparation time: 20 minutes
Cooking time: 0 minutes
Servings: 4
Ingredients:

- 1 pound (454 g) sushi-grade ahi tuna, cut into 1-inch cubes
- 3 scallions, thinly sliced
- 1 serrano chile, seeded and minced (optional)
- 3 tablespoons coconut aminos
- 1 teaspoon rice vinegar
- 1 teaspoon sesame oil
- 1 teaspoon toasted sesame seeds
- Dash ground ginger
- 1 large avocado, diced
- 1 cucumber, sliced into ½-inch-thick rounds

Directions:

1. In a large bowl, gently mix the first eight ingredients until well combined.
2. Cover and refrigerate to marinate for 15 minutes.
3. Stir in the avocado, gently incorporating the chunks into the ahi mixture.
4. Arrange the cucumber slices on a plate.
5. Place a spoonful of the ahi poke on each cucumber slice and serve immediately.

Per serving: Calories: 214kcal; Fat: 15g; Protein: 10g; Carbs: 11g

CHAPTER 5: Meat Recipes

61. Yellow Chicken Curry

Preparation time: 10 minutes
Cooking time: 35 minutes
Servings: 6
Ingredients:

- 2 tablespoons coconut oil
- 2 (4-ounce) boneless chicken breasts, cut into bite-size pieces
- 6 garlic cloves, minced
- 2 medium carrots, diced
- 1 small white onion, diced
- 1 tablespoon minced peeled fresh ginger
- 1 cup sugar snap peas, diced
- 1 cup chicken broth
- ½ cup canned diced tomatoes, with their juice
- 1 (5.4-ounce) can of unsweetened coconut cream
- ¼ cup filtered water
- 1 tablespoon fish sauce
- 1 tablespoon Indian curry powder
- ¼ teaspoon salt
- Pinch cayenne pepper
- Black pepper

Directions:

1. Heat 1 tablespoon of coconut oil over medium-high heat in a suitable skillet. Add the chicken and cook for almost 15 minutes, until cooked through. Set aside.
2. Heat the remaining 1 tablespoon of coconut oil in another large skillet over medium heat. Add the garlic, carrots, onion, ginger, and sauté for 5 minutes or until the onions soften.
3. Stir in the snap peas, broth, tomatoes, coconut cream, water, fish sauce, curry powder, salt, and cayenne pepper, and season with black pepper. Bring to a simmer, Reduce its heat to medium-low, and cook for 10 minutes.
4. Add the cooked chicken and cook for 2 minutes until reheated.
5. Serve hot over rice or quinoa, if desired.

Per serving: Calories: 441kcal; Fat: 33.9g; Protein: 21.4g; Carbs: 14.9g

62. Chicken Bites with Aioli

Preparation time: 10 minutes
Cooking time: 10 minutes
Servings: 4
Ingredients:

For the aioli

- ½ cup paleo mayonnaise
- 1 tablespoon lemon juice
- ¼ teaspoon garlic powder
- Dash cayenne pepper
- Dash salt

For the chicken

- 1 pound boneless chicken breast, diced
- 2 tablespoons avocado oil
- ½ teaspoon salt
- ½ teaspoon garlic powder

Directions:

1. To make the aioli:
2. Mix the mayonnaise, lemon juice, garlic powder, cayenne, and salt in a suitable bowl.
3. To make the chicken:
4. Preheat your broiler.

5. Layer a baking sheet with aluminum foil.

6. Spread out the chicken pieces on a plate. Brush with the avocado oil, and sprinkle with salt and garlic powder.

7. Arrange the chicken on the prepared pan so the pieces are not touching. Broil the chicken for 7 to 10 minutes, turning halfway through.

8. Serve the chicken bites alongside the aioli sauce for dipping.

Per serving: Calories: 238kcal; Fat: 10.6g; Protein: 33g; Carbs: 0.6g

63. Chicken Salad with Green Apples and Grapes

Preparation time: 15 minutes
Cooking time: 0
Servings: 4
Ingredients:

- 1 large avocado, diced
- 2 tablespoons Dijon mustard
- ½ teaspoon garlic powder
- Dash salt
- Dash black pepper
- 2 (8-ounce) grilled boneless, skinless chicken breasts, chopped
- 2 small green apples, diced
- 1 cup grapes, halved
- ¼ cup sliced scallions
- 2 tablespoons minced celery

Directions:

1. Add the avocado, mustard, garlic powder, salt, and pepper to a suitable bowl, stirring until creamy.

2. Add the chicken, apples, grapes, scallions, and celery. Stir well to combine.

3. Serve chilled, if desired.

Per serving: Calories: 314kcal; Fat: 13.3g; Protein: 26g; Carbs: 24.9g

64. Baked Chicken Breast with Lemon & Garlic

Preparation time: 5 minutes
Cooking time: 20 to 25 minutes
Servings: 4
Ingredients:

- Juice of 1 lemon
- Zest of 1 lemon
- 1 teaspoon garlic powder
- ½ teaspoon salt
- 3 tablespoons avocado oil
- 2 (8-ounce) boneless, skinless chicken breasts

Directions:

1. At 375 degrees F, preheat your oven.

2. Mix the lemon juice, lemon zest, garlic powder, and salt in a suitable bowl. Set aside.

3. With a basting brush, spread 1½ tablespoons of avocado oil on the bottom of a glass or ceramic baking dish and brush them with the chicken breasts in the container. Brush the remaining 1½ tablespoons of avocado oil.

4. With the brush, coat the chicken with the lemon-garlic mixture.

5. Bake for almost 20 to 25 minutes until the chicken reaches an internal temperature of 165 degrees F.

6. Serve.

Per serving: Calories: 232kcal; Fat: 9.7g; Protein: 33.1g; Carbs: 1.1g

65. Chicken Lettuce Wraps

Preparation time: 20 minutes
Cooking time: 0
Servings: 4
Ingredients:

- 2 heads of butter lettuce
- 1 pound grilled boneless chicken breast, cut into ½-inch cubes
- 1 cup shredded carrots
- ½ cup thinly sliced radishes
- 2 scallions, sliced thin
- 2 tablespoons chopped fresh cilantro
- ½ cup toasted sesame oil
- 3 tablespoons lime juice
- 1 tablespoon coconut aminos
- 1 garlic clove
- 1 thin slice of fresh ginger
- 1 teaspoon lime zest
- 1 tablespoon sesame seeds

Directions:

1. Place all the lettuce cups on a serving platter.
2. Divide the chicken, carrots, radishes, onions, and cilantro among the lettuce cups into an even layer.
3. In a suitable blender, combine the sesame oil, lime juice, coconut aminos, garlic, ginger, and lime zest. Blend until smooth.
4. Drizzle the chicken and vegetables with the dressing and sprinkle each with sesame seeds.

Per serving: Calories: 342kcal; Fat: 30g; Protein: 7g; Carbs: 13g

66. Pork Chops with Applesauce

Preparation time: 10 minutes
Cooking time: 15 minutes
Servings: 4
Ingredients:

- 4 thin-cut pork chops
- ½ teaspoon sea salt
- ⅛ teaspoon black pepper
- 6 apples, peeled, cored, and chopped
- ¼ cup packed brown sugar
- ¼ cup water
- 1 tablespoon grated fresh ginger

Directions:

1. At 425 degrees F, preheat your oven.
2. Season the pork chops with black pepper and salt, and put them on a rimmed baking sheet. Bake them for almost 15 minutes until the pork registers an internal temperature of 165 degrees F on an instant-read meat thermometer.
3. While baking the pork chops, stir together the apples, brown sugar, water, and ginger in a suitable pot over medium-high heat. Cover and cook for almost 10 minutes, occasionally stirring, until the apples have cooked into a sauce.
4. Serve the pork chops with the sauce.

Per serving: Calories: 338kcal; Fat: 3.6g; Protein: 22.9g; Carbs: 56.1g

67. Pork Chops with Kale

Preparation time: 10 minutes
Cooking time: 15 minutes
Servings: 4
Ingredients:

- 4 thin-cut pork chops
- 1 teaspoon sea salt
- ¼ teaspoon black pepper

- 4 tablespoons Dijon mustard
- 3 tablespoons olive oil
- ½ red onion, chopped
- 4 cups stemmed and chopped kale
- 2 tablespoons apple cider vinegar

Directions:

1. At 425 degrees F, preheat your oven.
2. Season the pork chops with ½ teaspoon salt and ⅛ teaspoon of pepper. Spread 2 tablespoons of the mustard over them and put them on a rimmed baking sheet. Bake for almost 15 minutes until the pork registers an internal temperature of 165 degrees F on an instant-read meat thermometer.
3. While the pork cooks heat the olive oil in a suitable skillet over medium-high until it shimmers.
4. Add the red onion and kale. Cook for almost 7 minutes, occasionally stirring, until the vegetables soften.
5. In a suitable bowl, whisk the rest of the 2 tablespoons of mustard, the cider vinegar, the rest of the ½ teaspoon of salt, and the rest of the ⅛ teaspoon of pepper. Add this to the kale. Cook for almost 2 minutes, while stirring.

Per serving: Calories: 235kcal; Fat: 16.6g; Protein: 13.5g; Carbs: 9.7g

68. Mustard Pork Tenderloin

Preparation time: 10 minutes
Cooking time: 15 minutes
Servings: 4
Ingredients:

- ½ cup fresh parsley leaves
- ¼ cup Dijon mustard
- 6 garlic cloves
- 3 tablespoons fresh rosemary leaves
- 3 tablespoons olive oil
- ½ teaspoon sea salt
- ¼ teaspoon black pepper
- 1 (1½-pound) pork tenderloin

Directions:

1. At 400 degrees F, preheat your oven.
2. In a suitable blender, combine the parsley, mustard, garlic, rosemary, olive oil, salt, and pepper. Pulse in 1-second pulses, about 20 times, until paste forms. Rub this paste all over the tenderloin and put the pork on a rimmed baking sheet.
3. Bake the pork for almost 15 minutes until it registers 165 degrees F on an instant-read meat thermometer.
4. Let rest for almost 5 minutes, slice, and serve.

Per serving: Calories: 362kcal; Fat: 17.6g; Protein: 45.8g; Carbs: 4.5g

69. Beef Steak Tacos

Preparation time: 10 minutes
Cooking time: 14 minutes
Servings: 4
Ingredients:

- ¼ cup fresh cilantro leaves
- 6 tablespoons olive oil
- 4 garlic cloves, minced
- 1 jalapeño pepper, chopped
- 1½ pounds beef flank steak
- ½ teaspoon sea salt
- ⅛ teaspoon black pepper
- Jalapeno guacamole sauce

Directions:

1. In a suitable blender or food processor, combine the cilantro and 4 tablespoons of olive oil, garlic, and jalapeño. Pulse 10 to 20 (1-second) pulses to make a paste. Set aside 1 tablespoon of the paste and spread the remainder over the flank steak. Let it rest for almost 5 minutes.

2. In a suitable skillet, heat the rest olive oil over medium-high heat until it shimmers.
3. Add the steak and cook it for almost 7 minutes on each side until it registers an internal temperature of 125 degrees F.
4. Transfer the cooked steak to a cutting board and let rest for almost 5 minutes. Slice it against the grain into ½-inch-thick slices. Set the pieces in a suitable bowl and toss with the reserved 1 tablespoon of herb paste.
5. Serve with the guacamole sauce.

Per serving: Calories: 502kcal; Fat: 31.7g; Protein: 51.9g; Carbs: 1.2g

70. Rosemary Lamb Chops

Preparation time: 15 minutes
Cooking time: 7-8 hours
Servings: 4
Ingredients:

- 1 medium onion, sliced
- 2 teaspoons garlic powder
- 2 teaspoons dried rosemary
- 1 teaspoon sea salt
- ½ teaspoon dried thyme leaves
- Black pepper
- 8 bone-in lamb chops (about 3 pounds)
- 2 tablespoons balsamic vinegar

Directions:

1. Layer the bottom of your slow cooker with the onion slices.
2. In a suitable bowl, stir together the garlic powder, rosemary, salt, thyme, and pepper. Rub the chops evenly with the spice mixture and gently place them in the slow cooker.
3. Drizzle the vinegar over the top.
4. Cover your slow cooker with its lid. Slow cook for 8 hours and serve.

Per serving: Calories: 213kcal; Fat: 8.1g; Protein: 31.1g; Carbs: 2.8g

71. Beef and Bell Pepper Fajitas

Preparation time: 5 minutes
Cooking time: 10 minutes
Servings: 4
Ingredients:

- 3 tablespoons olive oil
- 1½ pounds flank steak, sliced
- 2 green bell peppers, sliced
- 1 onion, sliced
- 1 cup store-bought salsa
- 1 teaspoon garlic powder
- ½ teaspoon sea salt

Directions:

1. Heat the olive oil in a suitable skillet over medium-high heat until it shimmers.
2. Add the beef, bell peppers, and onion and cook them for almost 6 minutes until the beef browns, stirring occasionally.
3. Stir in the salsa, garlic powder, and salt. Cook for almost 3 minutes, stirring occasionally.

Per serving: Calories: 461kcal; Fat: 24.9g; Protein: 48.8g; Carbs: 9.6g

72. Fried Beef and Broccoli

Preparation time: 10 minutes
Cooking time: 10 minutes
Servings: 4
Ingredients:

- 2 tablespoons olive oil
- 1 pound flank steak, sliced
- 1 cup broccoli florets
- 1 cup sugar snap peas
- 1 zucchini, chopped
- ¼ cup stir-fry sauce

Directions:

1. Heat the olive oil over medium-high heat in a suitable skillet until it shimmers.
2. Add the beef and cook for almost 5 to 7 minutes, occasionally stirring, until it browns. Remove with a slotted spoon and keep it aside on a platter.
3. Add the broccoli, sugar snap peas, and zucchini. Cook for almost 5 minutes, occasionally stirring, until the vegetables are crisp-tender.
4. Return the beef to this pan. Add the stir-fry sauce. Cook for almost 3 minutes, while stirring, until heated through.

Per serving: Calories: 318kcal; Fat: 17.3g; Protein: 33.5g; Carbs: 6.7g

73. Macadamia-Dusted Pork Cutlets

Preparation time: 10 minutes
Cooking time: 10 minutes
Servings: 4
Ingredients:

- 1 (1-pound) pork tenderloin, cut into ½-inch slices and pounded
- 1 teaspoon sea salt
- ¼ teaspoon black pepper
- ½ cup macadamia nuts, crushed
- 1 cup full-fat coconut milk
- 2 tablespoons olive oil

Directions:

1. At 400 degrees F, preheat your oven.
2. Season the pork chops with ½ teaspoon salt and ⅛ teaspoon of pepper.
3. In a shallow dish, mix up the macadamia nut powder, the rest of the ½ teaspoon of salt, and the rest of the ⅛ teaspoon of pepper.
4. Whisk the coconut milk and olive oil in another shallow dish to combine.

5. Dip the pork into the coconut milk and the macadamia nut powder. Put it on a rimmed baking sheet. Repeat with the rest of the pork slices.
6. Bake the pork for almost 10 minutes until it registers an internal temperature of 165 degrees F measured on an instant-read meat thermometer.

Per serving: Calories: 364kcal; Fat: 23.8g; Protein: 32.2g; Carbs: 6.2g

74. Lamb Meatballs with Sauce

Preparation time: 15 minutes
Cooking time: 7-8 hours
Servings: 6
Ingredients:

- 1½ pounds ground lamb
- 1 small white onion, minced
- 1 large egg
- 1 teaspoon garlic powder
- ½ teaspoon sea salt
- ½ teaspoon ground cumin
- ½ teaspoon pumpkin pie spice
- ½ teaspoon paprika
- ¼ teaspoon black pepper
- 1 cup avocado-dill sauce

Directions:

1. In a suitable bowl, combine the lamb, onion, egg, garlic powder, salt, cumin, pumpkin pie spice, paprika, and pepper.
2. Form the lamb mixture into about 12 meatballs. Arrange the meatballs along the bottom of your slow cooker.
3. Cover the cooker and set it on low. Cook for 7 to 8 hours.
4. Serve with the avocado-dill sauce.

Per serving: Calories: 115kcal; Fat: 4.6g; Protein: 16.6g; Carbs: 0.9g

75. Lamb Burgers with Herbed Yogurt Sauce

Preparation time: 40 minutes
Cooking time: 20 minutes
Servings: 6
Ingredients:

- Pickled onions
- ½ red onion, sliced
- 6 tablespoon lime juice
- ½ teaspoon kosher salt
- ½ teaspoon raw cane sugar
- Herbed yoghurt sauce
- 2 tablespoon lemon juice
- 1 cup Greek yogurt
- 1 garlic clove, minced
- 2 tablespoon chopped herbs
- Kosher salt
- Lamb burgers
- 1 tablespoon olive oil
- ½ red onion, diced
- 1 lb. Ground lamb
- 8 oz. Ground pork
- 3 tablespoon chopped mint
- 2 tablespoon chopped dill
- 3 tablespoon chopped parsley
- 4 garlic cloves, minced
- 1-½ teaspoons ground cumin
- 1 teaspoon ground coriander
- 1 teaspoon kosher salt
- ½ teaspoon black pepper
- Mixed greens, sliced tomatoes

Directions:

1. Mix the onion, lime juice, salt, and sugar in a suitable bowl.
2. Cover, and let the onions sit at room temperature for almost 2 hours.
3. In a suitable bowl, stir together the lemon juice, yogurt, garlic, herbs, and ½ teaspoon of salt. Cover and refrigerate this yogurt sauce until ready to use.
4. To make the lamb burgers: Warm the olive oil in a suitable skillet over medium heat.
5. Add the onion and cook for 7 minutes, frequently stirring, until softened. Transfer to a small plate to cool.
6. In a suitable bowl, combine the pork, lamb, dill, parsley, garlic, cumin, mint, coriander, salt, pepper, and cooled onions.
7. Form the mixture into six equal-sized meatballs. Press each into a patty and transfer to a parchment-lined baking sheet.
8. Prepare a suitable grill for cooking over medium-high heat.
9. Lightly grease its grill grate. Place the burgers on the preheated grill, and cook for 5 minutes per side.
10. Place the burgers on a platter and let them aside for 5 minutes before serving.
11. Serve with a big dollop of herbed yoghurt sauce and pickled onions.
12. Greens and sliced tomatoes or cucumbers are optional. Serve.

Per serving: Calories: 351kcal; Fat: 20.6g; Protein: 35.7g; Carbs: 5.4g

CHAPTER 6: Stews and Soups

76. Spicy Pumpkin Soup

Preparation time: 10 minutes
Cooking time: 45 minutes
Servings: 5
Ingredients:

- 2 cups of lentils
- 2 cups of squash
- 2 tomatoes
- 3 cups low sodium vegetable broth
- 2 red onions
- 6 leaves of dill
- 6 basil leaves
- 1 pinch of salt
- 2 tablespoons of olive oil
- 1 pinch of salt
- 1 pinch of cayenne pepper
- 1 chili
- 2 cloves of garlic

Directions:
1. Cut the tomato into cubes, and chop the onion with the chili. In a saucepan, fry the onion and add the tomato. Cook for 5 minutes.
2. Add the broth, lentils, salt, pepper, and garlic, and cook for 40 minutes.
3. Coarsely chop the dill and basil leaves, add them to the soup and cook for the last 5 minutes.
4. The soup can be eaten like this or pureed.

Per serving: Calories: 133kcal; Fat: 6g; Protein: 6g; Carbs: 17g

77. Orange Soup

Preparation time: 12 minutes
Cooking time: 45 minutes

Servings: 4
Ingredients:

- 2 cups of carrots
- 2 cups of squash
- 2 sweet potatoes
- 1 grated ginger root
- 2 cups of low sodium vegetable broth
- 1 cup unsweetened coconut milk
- 1 teaspoon of paprika
- 7 basil leaves
- 1 pinch of salt
- 2 tablespoons of olive oil
- 1 pinch of salt
- 1 pinch of cayenne pepper

Directions:
1. Chop the basil leaves in a pan with the oil and paprika.
2. Dice the sweet potatoes, pumpkin, and carrots, and sauté for 5 minutes, stirring with a spoon.
3. Add the broth, coconut milk, salt, pepper, and ginger.
4. Boil for 45 minutes over moderate heat. Serve hot.

Per serving: Calories: 155kcal; Fat: 8g; Protein: 3g; Carbs: 20g

78. Lentils And Turmeric Soup

Preparation time: 10 minutes
Cooking time: 25 minutes
Servings: 3
Ingredients:

- 2 cups of boiled lentils
- 2 carrots
- 1 shallot

- 1 tablespoon of turmeric
- 1 cup unsweetened almond milk
- 1 cup low sodium vegetable broth
- 1 clove of garlic
- 1 teaspoon of parsley
- 1/2 cup unsweetened soy yogurt
- 1 pinch of salt
- 2 tablespoons of ghee
- 1 pinch of salt
- 1 pinch of cayenne pepper
- 1 tablespoon of sesame seeds

Directions:

1. Wash and cut the carrots into pieces.
2. Chop the shallot. Chop the garlic together with the parsley.
3. Put the ghee in a saucepan and sauté the garlic and parsley for 1 minute.
4. Add the lentils and carrots and sauté for 5 minutes.
5. Add the cup of almond milk and the cup of broth, turmeric, salt and pepper, and shallot.
6. Cook over moderate heat for 25 minutes.
7. Serve with the sesame seeds.

Per serving: Calories: 249kcal; Fat: 4g; Protein: 16g; Carbs: 41g

79. Buckwheat Soup And Onions

Preparation time: 10 minutes
Cooking time: 20 minutes
Servings: 3
Ingredients:

- 2 cups of red onions
- 2 sweet potatoes
- 1/2 cup of buckwheat
- 1 shallot
- 1 tablespoon of thyme
- 2 cups unsweetened coconut milk
- 3 cup low sodium vegetable broth
- 1 clove of garlic
- 1 pinch of salt
- 3 tablespoons of olive oil
- 1 pinch of salt
- 1 pinch of cayenne pepper

Directions:

1. Chop the garlic with the onions and the shallot.
2. In a pan, brown the diced potatoes with the chopped onions and garlic for 5 minutes, adding the thyme.
3. Add the coconut milk, salt, and pepper, the vegetable broth and bring to a boil, add the buckwheat and cook over moderate heat for about 20 minutes.
4. The soup can be enjoyed like this or pureed.

Per serving: Calories: 389kcal; Fat: 18g; Protein: 8g; Carbs: 49g

80. Chestnut And Bean Soup

Preparation time: 5 minutes
Cooking time: 25 minutes
Servings: 3
Ingredients:

- 2 cups low sodium vegetable broth
- 1 cup unsweetened hazelnut milk
- 2 cups of boiled green beans
- 1 yellow onion
- 1 1/3 cups of boiled chestnuts
- 1 teaspoon of rosemary
- 1 pinch of salt
- 2 tablespoons of coconut oil
- 1 pinch of cayenne pepper
- 10 hazelnuts

Directions:

1. Boil the chestnuts and remove the peel, and chop.

2. Chop the onion and rosemary and brown them in a saucepan with coconut oil.

3. Add the boiled and chopped green beans, and add salt and pepper.

4. Cook for 5 minutes, stirring with a spoon. Add the chestnuts, hazelnut milk, and broth and cook over medium heat for about 20 minutes.

5. Serve the soup hot with the chopped hazelnuts.

Per serving: Calories: 184kcal; Fat: 6g; Protein: 5g; Carbs: 28g

81. Turnip And Spelled Soup

Preparation time: 10 minutes
Cooking time: 25 minutes
Servings: 3
Ingredients:

- 3 cups low sodium vegetable broth
- 1 cup of unsweetened soy milk
- 1 1/3 lb of turnip
- 1 red onion
- 1 cup of spelled
- 1 teaspoon of thyme
- 1 pinch of salt
- 2 tablespoons of olive oil
- 1 pinch of cayenne pepper
- 1 teaspoon of turmeric

Directions:

1. Chop the onion and brown it in the olive oil together with the thyme.

2. Add the diced turnip, salt, and pepper.

3. Add the cup of soy and half a cup of vegetable stock, cover, and cook for 15 minutes over moderate heat.

4. In another saucepan, bring the remaining vegetable broth with the turmeric to a boil and cook the spelled for about 20 minutes.

5. Blend the turnip, drain the farro well and mix.

6. Serve the creamy soup hot.

Per serving: Calories: 199kcal; Fat: 14g; Protein: 7g; Carbs: 17g

82. Spinach And Kale Soup

Preparation time: 5 minutes
Cooking time: 30 minutes
Servings: 4
Ingredients:

- 3 cups of spinach
- 3 cups of kale
- 1 sweet potato
- 1 yellow onion
- 4 cups low sodium vegetable broth
- 1 cup of unsweetened soy milk
- 2 tablespoons of olive oil
- 1 pinch of cayenne pepper
- 2 tablespoons of hemp seeds

Directions:

1. Bring the vegetable broth and soy milk to a boil, and add the spinach, kale, peeled and diced sweet potato, salt, and pepper.

2. Cook over medium heat for about 30 minutes.

3. Transfer to a mixer and blend well. Serve hot with the hemp seeds.

Per serving: Calories: 153kcal; Fat: 11g; Protein: 6g; Carbs: 12g

83. Soup Of Mushrooms And Tempeh

Preparation time: 5 minutes
Cooking time: 25 minutes
Servings: 3
Ingredients:

- 1 1/3 lb of cremini mushrooms
- 1/2 cup of tempeh
- 2 yellow onions

- 5 cups low sodium vegetable broth
- 3 tablespoons of rice flour
- 1 tablespoon of parsley
- 1 pinch of black pepper
- 1 pinch of salt
- 2 tablespoons of olive oil

Directions:

1. Clean the mushrooms and cut them.
2. Put the olive oil in a saucepan with the chopped onions and parsley and brown them for 5 minutes.
3. Add the vegetable broth and the diced tempeh and cook for about 25 minutes.
4. Add the rice flour and mix for 5 minutes.
5. Transfer all the ingredients to a mixer and blend until creamy.

Per serving: Calories: 206kcal; Fat: 13g; Protein: 13g; Carbs: 15g

84. Seitan Stew With Olives

Preparation time: 5 minutes
Cooking time: 20 minutes
Servings: 6
Ingredients:

- 14 ounces of seitan
- 1 carrot
- 1 red onion
- 2 stalks of celery
- 2 cloves of garlic
- 1 cup of tomato puree
- 1 tablespoon of goji berries
- 2 tablespoons of Italian seasoning
- 1 pinch of salt
- 1 pinch of cayenne pepper
- 1 teaspoon of curry
- 2 tablespoons of olive oil
- 10 black olives

Directions:

1. Chop the carrot, the garlic with the celery stalks, and the onion and brown in a non-stick pan with olive oil.
2. Add the chopped seitan, salt, and pepper, cook for 5 minutes, stirring, and then add the tomato sauce, a couple of tablespoons of boiling water, the Italian seasoning, curry, and berries, and cook for about 10 more minutes.
3. Add the black olives and serve hot.

Per serving: Calories: 239kcal; Fat: 6g; Protein: 17g; Carbs: 9g

85. Fennel Pear Soup

Preparation time: 10 minutes
Cooking time: 15 minutes
Servings: 4
Ingredients:

- 2 tablespoons extra-virgin olive oil
- 2 leeks, white part only, sliced
- 1 fennel bulb, cut into ¼-inch-thick slices
- 2 pears, peeled, cored, and cut into ½-inch cubes
- 1 teaspoon salt
- ¼ teaspoon black pepper
- ½ cup cashews
- 3 cups water or vegetable broth
- 2 cups spinach or arugula

Directions:

1. Heat the olive oil in a suitable Dutch oven over high heat.
2. Add the leeks and fennel. Sauté for 5 minutes.
3. Add the pears, salt, and pepper. Sauté for 3 minutes more.
4. Add the cashews and water and bring the soup to a boil. Reduce its heat to

simmer and cook for 5 minutes, partially covered.

5. Stir in the spinach.
6. Pour the prepared soup into a blender, working in batches if necessary, and purée until smooth.

Per serving: Calories: 229kcal; Fat: 12.6g; Protein: 5.4g; Carbs: 26.2g

86. Lentil and Carrot Soup

Preparation time: 15 minutes
Cooking time: 10 minutes
Servings: 4 to 6
Ingredients:

- 1 tablespoon coconut oil
- 2 carrots, sliced thin
- 1 small white onion, peeled and sliced thin
- 2 garlic cloves, peeled and sliced thin
- 1 tablespoon chopped fresh ginger
- 3 cups water or vegetable broth
- 1 (15-ounce) can of lentils, drained and rinsed
- 2 tablespoons chopped fresh cilantro or parsley
- 1 teaspoon salt
- ¼ teaspoon black pepper

Directions:

1. In a suitable pot over medium-high heat, melt the coconut oil. Add the carrots, onion, garlic, and ginger. Sauté for 5 minutes.
2. Add the water to the pot and bring it to a boil. Reduce its heat to simmer and cook for almost 5 minutes, or until the carrots are tender.
3. Add the lentils, cilantro, salt, and pepper. Stir well, and serve.

Per serving: Calories: 307kcal; Fat: 3.8g; Protein: 21.2g; Carbs: 47.2g

87. Roasted Vegetable Soup

Preparation time: 30 minutes
Cooking time: 40 minutes
Servings: 6 to 8
Ingredients:

- 4 carrots, halved lengthwise
- ½ head cauliflower, broken into florets
- 2 cups cubed butternut squash
- 3 shallots, halved lengthwise
- 3 Roma tomatoes, quartered
- 4 garlic cloves
- ½ cup extra-virgin olive oil
- 1 teaspoon salt
- ¼ teaspoon black pepper
- 4 to 6 cups of water or vegetable broth

Directions:

1. At 400 degrees F, preheat your oven.
2. Combine the carrots, cauliflower, butternut squash, shallots, tomatoes, and garlic in a suitable bowl. Add the olive oil, salt, and pepper and toss well.
3. Arrange all the vegetables in a rimmed baking sheet in a single layer.
4. Place this sheet in the preheated oven, and roast all the vegetables for almost 25 minutes or until they start to brown.
5. Transfer the roasted vegetables to a suitable Dutch oven over high heat.
6. Pour in enough water to cover the vegetables and cook to a boil.
7. Reduce its heat to a simmer and then continue cooking for almost 10 minutes on a simmer.
8. Pour the prepared soup into a blender, working in batches if necessary, and purée until smooth.

Per serving: Calories: 197kcal; Fat: 17g; Protein: 1.9g; Carbs: 12.5g

88. Sweet Potato and Rice Soup

Preparation time: 15 minutes
Cooking time: 15 minutes
Servings: 4 to 6
Ingredients:

- 4 cups vegetable broth
- 1 sweet potato, peeled and diced
- 2 onions, chopped
- 2 garlic cloves, sliced thin
- 2 teaspoons minced fresh ginger
- 1 bunch broccolini, cut into 1-inch pieces
- 1 cup cooked basmati rice
- ¼ cup fresh cilantro leaves

Directions:

1. In a suitable Dutch oven over high heat, add the broth and bring it to a boil.
2. Add the sweet potato, onion, garlic, and ginger. Simmer for 5 to 8 minutes or until the sweet potato is cooked.
3. Add the broccolini and simmer for an additional 3 minutes.
4. Remove this pan from the heat. Stir in the rice and cilantro.

Per serving: Calories: 186kcal; Fat: 1.3g; Protein: 6.8g; Carbs: 36.2g

89. Chicken Noodle Soup

Preparation time: 10 minutes.
Cooking time: 25 minutes.
Servings: 4
Ingredients:

- ¼ cup extra-virgin olive oil
- 3 celery stalks, cut into ¼-inch slices
- 2 medium carrots, cut into ¼-inch dice
- 1 small onion, cut into ¼-inch dice
- 1 fresh rosemary sprig
- 4 cups chicken broth
- 8 ounces gluten-free penne

- 1 teaspoon salt
- ¼ teaspoon black pepper, freshly ground
- 2 cups diced rotisserie chicken
- ¼ cup chopped fresh flat-leaf parsley

Directions:

1. In a suitable pot, heat the oil over high heat.
2. Add the celery, carrots, onion, rosemary, and sauté until softened for 5 to 7 minutes.
3. Add the broth, penne, salt, and pepper, and bring to a boil.
4. Reduce its heat to a simmer and cook until the penne is tender 8 to 10 minutes.
5. Remove and discard the rosemary sprig, and add the chicken and parsley.
6. Reduce its heat to low. Cook until the chicken is warmed, about 5 minutes, and serve.

Per serving: Calories: 302kcal; Fat: 14.7g; Protein: 24g; Carbs: 19.2g

90. Beefy Lentil Stew

Preparation time: 15 minutes
Cooking time: 10 minutes
Servings: 4
Ingredients:

- 2 tablespoons olive oil
- 1 pound extra-lean ground beef
- 1 onion, chopped
- 1 (14-ounce) can lentils, drained
- 1 (14-ounce) can of chopped tomatoes with garlic and basil, drained
- ½ teaspoon sea salt
- ⅛ teaspoon black pepper

Directions:

1. In your pot, heat the olive oil over medium-high heat until it shimmers.

2. Add the beef and onion, cook them for almost 5 minutes, crumbling the meat with a spoon until it browns.

3. Stir in the lentils, tomatoes, salt, and pepper. Bring to a simmer. Reduce its heat to medium. Cook for almost 3 to 4 minutes, while stirring until the lentils are hot.

Per serving: Calories: 487kcal; Fat: 13.5g; Protein: 47.4g; Carbs: 42.6g

CHAPTER 7: Snacks and Appetizers

91. Skewers Of Tofu And Zucchini

Preparation time: 5 minutes
Cooking time: 5 minutes
Servings: 6
Ingredients:

- 8 ounces of smoked tofu
- 2 courgettes
- 2 tablespoons of olive oil
- 1 pinch of salt
- 1 pinch of red pepper

Directions:

1. Cut the tofu into cubes and brown it for 5 minutes in a non-stick pan with a tablespoon of oil.
2. Cut the courgettes into slices, and with the help of a kitchen brush, grease them with the oil previously mixed with the salt and chili pepper.
3. Grill the courgettes without letting them burn.
4. Place a cube of tofu alternating with a slice of courgette on a skewer toothpick, and repeat.
5. Continue until all ingredients are consumed.

Per serving: Calories: 127kcal; Fat: 9g; Protein: 8g; Carbs: 4g

92. Rosti Potatoes With Rosemary

Preparation time: 5 minutes
Cooking time: 10 minutes
Servings: 3
Ingredients:

- 3 yellow potatoes
- 1 red onion
- 10 cashews
- 1 tablespoon of powdered rosemary
- 1 pinch of salt
- 1 pinch of cayenne pepper
- 2 tablespoons of olive oil

Directions:

1. Peel the potatoes and grate them.
2. Place them in a clean cloth and squeeze well to remove excess water.
3. Mix the potatoes with a pinch of salt, pepper, rosemary, chopped cashews, and onion.
4. Heat the oil in a non-stick pan and cook the dough in spoonfuls for 5 minutes per side.

Per serving: Calories: 287kcal; Fat: 12g; Protein: 5g; Carbs: 42g

93. Sweets With Carrots And Chocolate

Preparation time: 20 minutes
Cooking time: 25 minutes
Servings: 4
Ingredients:

- 4 tablespoons of maple syrup
- 3 tablespoons of wholemeal flour
- 3 tablespoons of almond flour
- 3 tablespoons of raw cocoa powder
- 1 teaspoon ground cinnamon
- the zest of an organic lemon
- 2 organic eggs
- 3 tablespoons of ghee
- 4 tablespoons of coconut milk
- ¾ cup of grated carrots
- 1 teaspoon of baking soda
- 1 teaspoon of cardamom
- 1 pinch of salt

Directions:

1. Mix the flour in a bowl with baking soda, cardamom, cocoa, cinnamon, and lemon zest.
2. Beat the eggs with coconut milk, carrots, salt, and maple syrup.
3. Combine the two compounds and mix well.
4. Fill the muffin tins three-quarters full and bake in a hot oven at 350° F for about 25 minutes.

Per serving: Calories: 214kcal; Fat: 13g; Protein: 8g; Carbs: 17g

94. Chestnut Panini With Fennels

Preparation time: 15 minutes
Cooking time: 30 minutes
Servings: 5
Ingredients:

- ¾ cups of boiled chestnuts
- 1 tablespoon of goji berries
- 1 tablespoon of olive oil
- 1 shallot
- ¾ cup of fennel
- 2 teaspoons of dried sage
- 2 teaspoons of organic lemon zest
- 1/2 cup of orange juice
- 3 tablespoons of grated quinoa bread (see recipe)
- 5 pecans with pellicle
- 1 organic egg
- 1 cup of blueberries

Directions:

1. Put the goji berries in a bowl of cold water for 10 minutes, and drain well.
2. In a non-stick pan, heat the oil and brown the shallot with the chopped fennel for 5 minutes. Add a few tablespoons of boiling water and continue cooking until soft.
3. Put the boiled chestnuts in a bowl, add the soaked goji berries, the browned fennel and shallot, the orange juice, the blueberries, the lemon zest, the chopped walnuts, and the beaten egg.
4. Grease a loaf pan with oil, then pour the dough.
5. Level with the back of a spoon soaked in cold water and sprinkle with grated quinoa bread.
6. Heat the oven to 350° F and bake for about 30 minutes. Cut into slices.

Per serving: Calories: 128kcal; Fat: 6g; Protein: 3g; Carbs: 92g

95. Oat Bars With Cocoa And Honey

Preparation time: 10 minutes
Cooking time: 10 minutes
Servings: 7
Ingredients:

- 15 tablespoons of oat flakes
- 12 tablespoons of pecans with pellicle
- 12 tablespoons of raw honey
- 2 tablespoons of natural cocoa

Directions:

1. Crumble the pecans and roast them for 2 minutes, constantly stirring, in a non-stick pan.
2. Mix the toasted walnuts in a bowl with honey, cocoa, and oats.
3. Spread the mixture on a baking sheet lined with parchment paper and cover it with another sheet of parchment paper.
4. Press lightly with a kitchen rolling pin.
5. Heat the baking tray to 320° F and bake after removing the top sheet.
6. Cook for about 10 minutes.
7. Remove from the oven, allow to cool, and cut into bars.

Per serving: Calories: 345kcal; Fat: 15g; Protein: 10g; Carbs: 46g

96. Turmeric Focaccia With Nuts

Preparation time: 10 minutes
Cooking time: 15 minutes
Servings: 6
Ingredients:

- 2 cups of spelled flour
- ½ cup of wholemeal flour
- 2 tablespoons of turmeric
- 3 tablespoons of walnuts
- 1 teaspoon of organic dry yeast
- 1 cup of water
- 1 pinch of salt
- 1 tablespoon of olive oil

Directions:

1. Combine the spelled flour, turmeric, wholemeal flour, chopped walnuts, salt, and dry yeast and mix. Slowly add the water and mix well.
2. Grease a pan with olive oil, pour the mixture, and bake at 400° F for about 15 minutes.

Per serving: Calories: 177kcal; Fat: 2g; Protein: 7g; Carbs: 34g

97. Pear And Cinnamon Pudding

Preparation time: 10 minutes
Cooking time: 0 minutes
Servings: 2
Ingredients:

- 2 pears
- 60 grams of low kcal; Fat: cottage cheese
- 1 organic lemon
- 1 tablespoon of maple syrup
- 1 tablespoon of ground cinnamon
- 1 tablespoon of chopped hazelnuts

Directions:

1. Peel the pears and dice them, squeeze the lemon juice, and put it in a bowl with the pears.
2. Add the syrup and mix well. Divide the mixture into two glasses and cover with the cottage cheese. Decorate with chopped hazelnuts.

Per serving: Calories: 115kcal; Fat: 0g; Protein: 1g; Carbs: 31g

98. Peanut Butter Toast With Vegetables

Preparation time: 10 minutes
Cooking time: 0 minutes
Servings: 2
Ingredients:

- 4 slices of wholemeal toast bread
- 1 tablespoon of peanut butter
- 1 cucumber
- 1 onion
- 1 tomato
- 1 tablespoon of chopped fresh basil

Directions:

1. Toast the toast without burning, and spread the peanut butter on two slices.
2. Peel the cucumber and cut it into slices, chop the onion, and wash and slice the tomato.
3. Put the cucumber slices on top of the buttered bread slices, add the tomato slices and the chopped onion and close the toast with the other pieces of bread.

Per serving: Calories: 220kcal; Fat: 5g; Protein: 8g; Carbs: 35g

99. Strawberries, Lemon And Mint

Preparation time: 10 minutes
Cooking time: 5 minutes
Servings: 3
Ingredients:

- 2 cups of strawberries

- 1 tablespoon of maple syrup
- 1 tablespoon of chopped fresh mint leaves
- 2 organic lemons
- ¾ cup of 70% dark chocolate

Directions:

1. Wash the strawberries and cut them into cubes.
2. Squeeze the lemon juice and mix it with maple syrup and mint.
3. Add the strawberries and leave them to flavor for a few minutes.
4. Meanwhile, melt the chocolate in a bain-marie.
5. Put the strawberries in three bowls and add the hot dark chocolate.

Per serving: Calories: 237kcal; Fat: 15g; Protein: 3g; Carbs: 24g

100. Oranges Stuffed With Banana And Blueberries

Preparation time: 10 minutes + 2 hours of rest
Cooking time: 0 minutes
Servings: 6
Ingredients:

- 3 oranges
- 1 cup of blueberries
- 2 bananas
- 2 tablespoons of maple syrup

Directions:

1. Peel the bananas and cut them into small pieces.
2. Mix the bananas with the blueberries and maple syrup in a bowl, place in an airtight bag, and place in the freezer for 2 hours.
3. Wash the oranges well, divide them in half, and empty the inner pulp with the help of a teaspoon. Put the oranges in the freezer as well.
4. After the two hours, put the bananas and blueberries in a mixer and blend well.
5. Stuff the oranges with the pureed fruit.

Per serving: Calories: 86kcal; Fat: 0g; Protein: 1g; Carbs: 22g

101. Citrus Spinach

Preparation time: 10 minutes
Cooking time: 7 minutes
Servings: 4
Ingredients:

- 2 tablespoons extra-virgin olive oil
- 4 cups fresh baby spinach
- 2 garlic cloves, minced
- Juice of ½ orange
- Zest of ½ orange
- ½ teaspoon sea salt
- ⅛ teaspoon black pepper

Directions:

1. Heat the olive oil in a suitable skillet over medium-high heat until it shimmers.
2. Toss in the spinach and cook for 3 minutes, stirring occasionally.
3. Add the garlic. Cook for 30 seconds, stirring constantly.
4. Add the orange juice, orange zest, salt, and pepper. Cook for almost 2 minutes, constantly stirring, until the liquid evaporates.

Per serving: Calories: 117kcal; Fat: 7.1g;g; Protein: 2 Carbs: 12.8g

102. Coconut Rice with Blueberries

Preparation time: 10 minutes
Cooking time: 30 minutes
Servings: 4
Ingredients:

- 1 cup brown basmati rice

- 2 dates, pitted and chopped
- 1 cup coconut milk
- 1 teaspoon sea salt
- 1 cup water
- ¼ cup toasted slivered almonds
- ½ cup shaved coconut
- 1 cup fresh blueberries

Directions:

1. Combine the basmati rice, dates, coconut milk, salt, and water in a saucepan. Stir to mix well. Bring to a boil.
2. Reduce its heat to low, then simmer for 30 minutes or until the rice is soft.
3. Divide them into four bowls and serve with almonds, coconut, and blueberries.

Per serving: Calories: 397kcal; Fat: 20g; Protein: 6.6g; Carbs: 50.8g

103. Almond–Stuffed Dates

Preparation time: 15 minutes
Cooking time: 2 minutes
Servings: 4–6
Ingredients:

- 20 Medjool dates
- 20 to 40 Marcona almonds
- 2 tablespoons olive oil
- 2 teaspoons grated orange zest
- ½ teaspoon fleur de sel

Directions:

1. Remove the pits from the dates. Gently stuff each date with 1 or 2 almonds, depending on the size of the date. Seal the almond inside by pressing the date around it.
2. In a suitable sauté pan over medium heat, heat the olive oil. Add the dates and gently sauté until warmed through, about 2 minutes.

3. Remove it from the heat and sprinkle with the orange zest and fleur de sel.
4. Serve or store in an airtight container in the refrigerator for up to 2 days.

Per serving: Calories: 197kcal; Fat: 16.8g; Protein: 6g; Carbs: 9.1g

104. Hummus with Pine Nuts

Preparation time: 20 minutes
Cooking time: 0 minutes
Servings: 6
Ingredients:

- 2 (15-oz) cans chickpeas, drained
- 3 tablespoons lemon juice
- 2 garlic cloves, crushed
- 2 teaspoons za'atar
- Kosher salt
- 1 cup water
- 4 tablespoons extra-virgin olive oil
- 3 tablespoons tahini
- 1 tablespoon pine nuts, toasted
- 1 teaspoon chopped parsley

Directions:

1. Blend the lemon juice, chickpeas, garlic, za'atar, and 1 ½ teaspoons salt in a suitable food processor.
2. Add ½ cup [120 ml] of the water, tahini, and 2 tablespoons of olive oil.
3. Blend until this mixture is creamy while pouring in ½ cup [120 ml] of the remaining water, 2 tablespoons at a time. Add lemon juice and salt to adjust the taste as you like.
4. Drizzle pine nuts, the remaining olive oil, and parsley on top to serve or store in an airtight container in the refrigerator for up to 2 weeks.

Per serving: Calories: 490kcal; Fat: 17.2g; Protein: 21.7g; Carbs: 66.2g

105. Chickpea and Garlic Hummus

Preparation time: 5 minutes
Cooking time: 0
Servings: 6
Ingredients:

- 3 garlic cloves, minced
- 2 tablespoons extra-virgin olive oil
- 2 tablespoons tahini
- 1 (14-ounce) can of chickpeas, drained
- Juice of 1 lemon
- ½ teaspoon sea salt
- Paprika, for garnish

Directions:

1. Combine garlic, olive oil, tahini, chickpeas, lemon juice, and salt in a suitable blender.
2. Blend until smooth.
3. Garnish as desired.

Per serving: Calories: 134kcal; Fat: 10.8g; Protein: 3.6g; Carbs: 8.6g

CHAPTER 8: Desserts

106. Chocolate And Cherries Cake

Preparation time: 10 minutes
Cooking time: 35 minutes
Servings: 8
Ingredients:

- 1 cup of pitted cherries
- 5 tablespoons of coconut milk
- 1 ¼ cups of wholemeal flour
- 1 ¼ cups of banana flour
- ¾ cup of raw cocoa
- 5 tablespoons of maple syrup
- 1 teaspoon of gluten-free, organic yeast
- 4 tablespoons of ghee
- 1 + 1/2 cup of oat milk

Directions:

1. Mix the wholemeal flour, banana flour, baking powder, and cocoa in a bowl.
2. Mix the maple syrup well with the ghee and oat milk in another bowl.
3. Mix the two compounds.
4. Heat the oven to 320° F.
5. Line a pan with parchment paper, pour the mixture and add the cherries.
6. Cook for about 35 minutes.

Per serving: Calories: 243kcal; Fat: 6g; Protein: 7g; Carbs: 44g

107. Yellow Cake

Preparation time: 10 minutes
Cooking time: 25 minutes
Servings: 5
Ingredients:

- 4 cups of oat milk
- 5 organic eggs
- 5 tablespoons of corn flour

- 5 tablespoons of maple syrup
- the zest of an organic orange

Directions:

1. Heat the milk and dissolve the maple syrup in it.
2. Beat the egg whites. Heat the oven to 400° F and line a pan with parchment paper.
3. Mix the cornmeal with the orange zest and warm milk in a bowl.
4. Pour into the pan and cook for about 25 minutes.

Per serving: Calories: 138kcal; Fat: 6g; Protein: 6g; Carbs: 16g

108. Beet Brownie

Preparation time: 10 minutes
Cooking time: 20 minutes
Servings: 8
Ingredients:

- 18 ounces of boiled beets
- 4 tablespoons of almond butter
- 1 ½ cups of 70% dark chocolate
- 3 organic eggs
- ¾ cup of buckwheat flour
- 1 tablespoon of raw cocoa
- 1 teaspoon of cardamom

Directions:

1. Beat the eggs with the sugar.
2. Put the well-drained beets with the chocolate and butter in the mixer and blend.
3. Add the beet mixture to the eggs and flour, and cocoa. Line a baking dish with parchment paper and pour the contents.
4. Bake at 350° F for about 20 minutes.

5. Cut into squares and serve.

Per serving: Calories: 334kcal; Fat: 18g; Protein: 12g; Carbs: 32g

109. Whole-meal Rice Pudding With Plums

Preparation time: 10 minutes
Cooking time: 25 minutes
Servings: 3
Ingredients:

- 1 cup of brown rice
- 4 cups of oat milk
- 1 tablespoon of maple syrup
- 1 pinch of salt
- 1 teaspoon of vanilla extract
- 2 organic eggs
- 5 dried and pitted plums

Directions:

1. Put the rice in the oat milk with the vanilla, salt, and syrup in a saucepan and cook over low heat.
2. Stir often. Cook until the milk is completely absorbed and the rice is soft. Remove from heat.
3. Beat eggs. Coarsely chop the plums.
4. Incorporate the eggs into the rice, add the prunes and return to the heat over low heat for 1 minute.

Per serving: Calories: 337kcal; Fat: 14g; Protein: 10g; Carbs: 6g

110. Pecan Walnut Pralines

Preparation time: 15 minutes
Cooking time: 0 minutes
Servings: 10
Ingredients:

- 3 tablespoons of maple syrup
- 3 tablespoons of grated coconut
- 1 teaspoon of vanilla extract
- 1 pinch of salt

- 3 tablespoons of almond butter
- 1 1/3 cups of pecans

Directions:

1. Place all ingredients except almond butter and grated coconut in the blender and blend on high speed for one minute.
2. Mix with the coconut butter and shape into balls with your hands. Pass the balls in the coconut.

Per serving: Calories: 148kcal; Fat: 13g; Protein: 2g; Carbs: 5g

111. Cookies With Peanut Butter And Sesame Seeds

Preparation time: 10 minutes
Cooking time: 8 minutes
Servings: 5
Ingredients:

- 1 ¼ cups of almond flour
- 1 ¼ cups of wholemeal flour
- 1 teaspoon of baking soda
- 1 teaspoon of raw cocoa
- 1 pinch of salt
- 5 tablespoons of peanut butter
- 3 tablespoons of sesame seeds
- 2 tablespoons of maple syrup
- 3 tablespoons of almond butter

Directions:

1. Mix the almond flour, wholemeal flour, baking soda, vanilla extract, salt, and cocoa.
2. Add the peanut butter, sesame seeds, maple syrup, and almond butter and knead.
3. Shape into balls with your hands and crush them.
4. Line a baking sheet with parchment paper, spread the cookies on the baking sheet, and bake at 330° F for about 8 minutes.

Per serving: Calories: 226kcal; Fat: 14g; Protein: 8g; Carbs: 17g

112. Baked Apples With Crumble

Preparation time: 10 minutes
Cooking time: 20 minutes
Servings: 16
Ingredients:

- 8 apples
- 1 teaspoon of grated ginger root
- 1 teaspoon of cinnamon
- 1 1/4 cups of pecans
- 1 1/3 cups of oat flakes
- 3 teaspoons of sesame
- 3 teaspoons of grated dried coconut
- 1 pinch of salt
- 5 tablespoons of ghee
- 5 tablespoons of maple syrup
- 2 organic lemons

Directions:

1. Peel and cut the apples into wedges.
2. Line a pan with parchment paper and distribute the apple wedges inside.
3. Squeeze the lemon juice, mix it with the cinnamon and ginger root and sprinkle over the apples.
4. Bake at 350° F for 10 minutes.
5. Meanwhile, mix the chopped pecans, coarsely chopped oat flakes in the blender, salt, maple syrup, ghee, sesame, and coconut in a bowl.
6. Make large crumbs with your hands, remove the apples from the oven and sprinkle the crumbs.
7. Bake again for about 10 minutes.

Per serving: Calories: 237kcal; Fat: 13g; Protein: 4g; Carbs: 30g

113. Ice Cream Cake With Raspberries

Preparation time: 15 minutes
Cooking time: 0 minutes
Servings: 8
Ingredients:

- 2 cups of raspberries
- 2 cups of peanut cookies (see recipe)
- 2 tablespoons of coconut butter
- 3 cups of coconut yogurt
- 1 tablespoon of maple syrup
- 1 tablespoon of 70% dark chocolate
- the juice of an organic lemon

Directions:

1. Blend the raspberries with maple syrup and lemon juice. Finely crumble the biscuits and mix them with the coconut butter.
2. Put the crumbled biscuits in a baking dish, and spread the yogurt mixed with the lampini sauce on top. Cover with chocolate and place in the freezer for a couple of hours.

Per serving: Calories: 287kcal; Fat: 22g; Protein: 7g; Carbs: 15g

114. Apricot Cake

Preparation time: 15 minutes
Cooking time: 25 minutes
Servings: 8
Ingredients:

- 2 cups of wholemeal flour
- 2 cups of almond flour
- 3/4 cup of rice milk
- 1 teaspoon of salt
- 1 tablespoon of chopped pecans
- 1 tablespoon of chopped hazelnuts
- 4 dried apricots cut into small pieces
- 4 tablespoons of almond butter

Directions:

1. Mix the two flours with the almond butter, the water, the milk, and the salt, mix well and let the dough rest in a cling film for about half an hour.
2. After this time, roll out the dough, put the pecans, hazelnuts and apricots in the center, and knead again. Leave to rest for 10 minutes.
3. Roll out the dough into a lightly greased ovenproof dish and bake in a hot oven at 350° F for about 25 minutes.

Per serving: Calories: 325kcal; Fat: 20g; Protein: 10g; Carbs: 25g

115. Pumpkin And Dates Cake

Preparation time: 15 minutes
Cooking time: 20 minutes
Servings: 8
Ingredients:

- ¾ cup of wholemeal flour
- 3 tablespoons of almond flour
- 4 cups boiled cubed squash
- 4 apples, peeled and cut into wedges
- 4 pitted dates
- 1 teaspoon of coconut butter

Directions:

1. Mix the flours. Put the pumpkin and dates in the blender and blend.
2. Mix the flour with the date and pumpkin cream.
3. Grease a pan, pour in the mixture, and decorate with the sliced apples standing in the dough.
4. Bake at 400° F for about 20 minutes.

Per serving: Calories: 170kcal; Fat: 4g; Protein: 4g; Carbs: 32g

116. Mint Chocolates

Preparation time: 15 minutes
Cooking time: 0 minutes
Servings: 20
Ingredients:

- 1 1/3 cups of dried and grated coconut
- 2/3 cup of almond flour
- 1 teaspoon of maple syrup
- 1 teaspoon of raw honey
- 1 cup of coconut oil
- 1 cup of ghee
- 2 tablespoons of 70% dark cocoa powder
- 2 tablespoons of powdered mint extract

Directions:

1. Mix and blend all the ingredients in the blender.
2. Pour the cream into chocolate molds and refrigerate for three hours.

Per serving: Calories: 186kcal; Fat: 16g; Protein: 2g; Carbs: 4g

117. Sorbet With Honey And Goji Berries

Preparation time: 15 minutes + 160 minutes waiting time
Cooking time: 0 minutes
Servings: 2
Ingredients:

- 5 tablespoons of raw honey
- 3 tablespoons of goji berries
- 1 cup of water

Directions:

1. Soak the goji berries for about 30 minutes, and drain well. Bring the cup of water to a boil and dissolve the honey.
2. Allow to cool, and add the goji berries.
3. Place in a container and place in the freezer for about 30 minutes.

4. Remove from the freezer, mix well, and put it back in the freezer for 30 minutes.
5. Repeat 5 times.

Per serving: Calories: 175kcal; Fat: 0g; Protein: 0g; Carbs: 47g

118. Peach Muffin

Preparation time: 10 minutes
Cooking time: 25 minutes
Servings: 4
Ingredients:

- 2 peeled and diced peaches
- 5 tablespoons of almond flour
- 5 tablespoons of wholemeal flour
- 3 tablespoons of agave syrup
- 2 cups of oats milk
- 3 tablespoons of coconut butter
- 1 teaspoon of organic yeast
- 2 organic eggs

Directions:

1. Mix the flour with the yeast.
2. Beat the eggs and stir in the coconut butter and agave syrup.
3. In a bowl, combine the milk with the flour and add the eggs.
4. Also, add the peaches.
5. Pour the mixture into the muffin molds, filling them three-quarters full.
6. Bake at 350° F for about 25 minutes.

Per serving: Calories: 381kcal; Fat: 19g; Protein: 12g; Carbs: 45g

119. Pears Cake

Preparation time: 10 minutes
Cooking time: 30 minutes
Servings: 6
Ingredients:

- 1 cup of buckwheat flour
- 1 cup of almond flour
- 28 ounces of peeled and diced pears
- 1 cup of coconut yogurt
- 3 tablespoons of rice flour
- 3 tablespoons of banana flour
- 3 tablespoons of water
- 5 tablespoons of maple syrup
- 1 teaspoon ground cinnamon
- 4 tablespoons of coconut oil
- 1 teaspoon of baking soda

Directions:

1. Mix all the flours with the cinnamon and baking soda.
2. Add the water and maple syrup, coconut oil, and yogurt, and mix well.
3. Finally, incorporate the pears. Line a pan with parchment paper and pour the dough. Bake in a hot oven at 350° F for about 30 minutes.

Per serving: Calories: 395kcal; Fat: 15g; Protein: 10g; Carbs: 59g

120. Stone Fruit Cobbler

Preparation time: 10 minutes
Cooking time: 20 minutes
Servings: 8
Ingredients:

- 1 teaspoon coconut oil plus ¼ cup melted
- 2 cups sliced fresh peaches
- 2 cups sliced fresh nectarines
- 2 tablespoons lemon juice
- ¾ cup almond flour
- ¾ cup rolled oats
- ¼ cup coconut sugar
- 1 teaspoon ground cinnamon
- ½ teaspoon vanilla extract
- Dash salt
- Filtered water for mixing

Directions:

1. At 425 degrees F, preheat your oven.
2. Coat the bottom of a suitable cast-iron skillet with 1 teaspoon coconut oil.
3. In the skillet, mix the peaches, nectarines, and lemon juice.
4. Add the almond flour, oats, coconut sugar, ¼ cup of melted coconut oil, cinnamon, vanilla, and salt in a suitable food processor or blender. Pulse until the oats are broken up and the mixture resembles a dry dough.
5. Pour the dough into a suitable bowl. With your fingers, break the dough into large chunks and sprinkle it across the top of the fruit.
6. Bake the food for 20 minutes. Serve warm.

Per serving: Calories: 110kcal; Fat: 3.4g; Protein: 3.1g; Carbs: 17.8g

30 Days Meal Plan

Day	Breakfast	Lunch	Dinner	Dessert
1	Mushroom Frittata	Beef Steak Tacos	Salmon With Rocket Pesto	Whole-meal Rice Pudding With Plums
2	Soy Cream With Asparagus	Basic Beans	Pork Chops With Kale	Chocolate And Cherries Cake
3	Pudding With Blackcurrant And Mint	Quinoa With Tuna Pesto	Lentil And Carrot Soup	Beet Brownie
4	Pistachio And Pecan Walnuts Granola For Breakfast	Mustard Pork Tenderloin	Bean And Spinach Casserole	Cookies With Peanut Butter And Sesame Seeds
5	Banana Date Porridge	Lamb Burgers With Herbed Yogurt Sauce	Cod With Creamy Onions	Pecan Walnut Pralines
6	Coconut Pancakes	Chipotle Kidney Bean Chili	Yellow Chicken Curry	Yellow Cake
7	Tofu Scramble	Whitefish Curry	Seaweed Fritters Nori And Carrots	Ice Cream Cake With Raspberries
8	Banana Oatmeal	Buckwheat Soup And Onions	Bean And Rice Casserole	Apricot Cake
9	Banana Pancakes With Apricots	Cod And Pumpkin Fishballs With White Sauce	Spinach And Kale Soup	Baked Apples With Crumble
10	Oat Flakes With Pears And Blueberries	Roasted Vegetable Soup	Ahi Poke With Cucumber	Pumpkin And Dates Cake
11	Quinoa Bread With Pecan Walnut Butter	Mushroom Risotto With Spring Peas	Beef And Bell Pepper Fajitas	Stone Fruit Cobbler
12	Crepes Of Chickpeas And Spinach	Mackerel With Sesame And Soy Sprouts	Macadamia-Dusted Pork Cutlets	Pears Cake
13	Millet Cake With Plums	Lamb Meatballs With Sauce	Spanish Rice	Sorbet With Honey And Goji Berries
14	Spicy Quinoa	Soup Of Oysters And Mushrooms	Chestnut And Bean Soup	Peach Muffin
15	Banana Muffin	Lentils And Turmeric Soup	Squid Rings With Saffron	Mint Chocolates

16	Banana Date Porridge	Herby Quinoa With Walnuts	Baked Chicken Breast With Lemon & Garlic	Pecan Walnut Pralines
17	Coconut Pancakes	Cabbage With Anchovies	Orange Soup	Yellow Cake
18	Banana Pancakes With Apricots	Fennel Pear Soup	Coconut Brown Rice	Baked Apples With Crumble
19	Mushroom Frittata	Indian Butter Chickpeas	Soup Of Mushrooms And Tempeh	Cookies With Peanut Butter And Sesame Seeds
20	Tofu Scramble	Turnip And Spelled Soup	Salmon Salad With Mushrooms And Broccoli	Ice Cream Cake With Raspberries
21	Banana Oatmeal	Brown Rice With Bell Peppers	Spicy Pumpkin Soup	Pumpkin And Dates Cake
22	Quinoa Bread With Pecan Walnut Butter	Coconut-Crusted Shrimp	Chicken Lettuce Wraps	Wholemeal Rice Pudding With Plums
23	Banana Muffin	Chicken Noodle Soup	Grandma's Black Bean Chili	Chocolate And Cherries Cake
24	Pistachio And Pecan Walnuts Granola For Breakfast	Chicken Salad With Green Apples And Grapes	Wholemeal Pasta With Sardines And Leeks	Sorbet With Honey And Goji Berries
25	Spicy Quinoa	Mediterranean Quinoa With Peperoncini	Rosemary Lamb Chops	Stone Fruit Cobbler
26	Pudding With Blackcurrant And Mint	Fish Sticks With Avocado Dipping Sauce	Sweet Potato And Rice Soup	Beet Brownie
27	Millet Cake With Plums	Seitan Stew With Olives	Curry Pastinache Cream With Leek And Black Beans	Mint Chocolates
28	Crepes Of Chickpeas And Spinach	Fried Beef And Broccoli	Chicken Bites With Aioli	Pears Cake
29	Soy Cream With Asparagus	Herbed Harvest Rice	Beefy Lentil Stew	Peach Muffin
30	Oat Flakes With Pears And Blueberries	Pork Chops With Applesauce	Southern Bean Bowl	Apricot Cake

Measurement Conversion Chart

Volume Equivalents (Liquid)

US Standard	US Standard (ounces)	Metric (approximate)
2 tablespoons	1 fl. oz.	30 mL
¼ cup	2 fl. oz.	60 mL
½ cup	4 fl. oz.	120 mL
1 cup	8 fl. oz.	240 mL
1½ cups	12 fl. oz.	355 mL
2 cups or 1 pint	16 fl. oz.	475 mL
4 cups or 1 quart	32 fl. oz.	1 L
1 gallon	128 fl. oz.	4 L

Volume Equivalents (Dry)

US Standard	Metric (approximate)
⅛ teaspoon	0.5 mL
¼ teaspoon	1 mL
½ teaspoon	2 mL
¾ teaspoon	4 mL
1 teaspoon	5 mL
1 tablespoon	15 mL
¼ cup	59 mL
⅓ cup	79 mL
½ cup	118 mL
⅔ cup	156 mL
¾ cup	177 mL
1 cup	235 mL
2 cups or 1 pint	475 mL
3 cups	700 mL
4 cups or 1 quart	1 L

Oven Temperatures

Fahrenheit (F)	Celsius (C) (approximate)
250°F	120°C
300°F	150°C
325°F	165°C
350°F	180°C
375°F	190°C
400°F	200°C
425°F	220°C

450°F	230°C

Weight Equivalents

US Standard	Metric (approximate)
½ ounce	15 g
1 ounce	30 g
2 ounces	60 g
4 ounces	115 g
8 ounces	225 g
12 ounces	340 g
16 ounces or 1 pound	455 g

Index

Potato Croquettes With Pumpkin Seeds; 30
Pudding With Blackcurrant And Mint; 21
Pumpkin And Dates Cake; 71
Quinoa Bread With Pecan Walnut Butter; 22
Quinoa With Tuna Pesto; 43
Roasted Broccoli and Cashews; 33
Roasted Vegetable Soup; 59
Rolls Of Quinoa Lettuce And Raspberries; 31
Rosemary Lamb Chops; 52
Rösti Potatoes With Rosemary; 62
Salmon Salad With Mushrooms And Broccoli; 42
Salmon With Rocket Pesto; 41
Salt Cake With Asparagus And Mushroom Cream;
    28
Seaweed Fritters Nori And Carrots; 44
Seitan Stew With Olives; 58
Skewers Of Tofu And Zucchini; 62
Sorbet With Honey And Goji Berries; 71
Soup Of Mushrooms And Tempeh; 57
Soup Of Oysters And Mushrooms; 43
Southern Bean Bowl; 38
Soy Cream With Asparagus; 22

Spanish Rice; 36
Spicy Pumpkin Soup; 55
Spicy Quinoa; 25
Spinach And Kale Soup; 57
Spinach With Leek And Hazelnuts; 29
Squid Rings With Saffron; 45
Stone Fruit Cobbler; 72
Strawberries, Lemon And Mint; 64
Sweet Potato and Rice Soup; 60
Sweet Potatoes In Sweet And Sour Sauce; 28
Sweets With Carrots And Chocolate; 62
Tempeh With Olives And Capers; 31
Tofu Scramble; 25
Turmeric Focaccia With Nuts; 64
Turnip And Spelled Soup; 57
Whitefish Curry; 46
Wholemeal Pasta With Sardines And Leeks; 41
Wholemeal Rice Pudding With Plums; 69
Yellow Cake; 68
Yellow Chicken Curry; 48
Zucchini Fritters With Garlic Sauce; 29

Conclusion

It's vital to incorporate anti-inflammatory foods into your diet to decrease the inflammation your body may be experiencing. An anti-inflammatory diet is an excellent option for someone who wants to improve their health. Still, it is also the perfect fit for anyone looking to incorporate anti-inflammatory foods into their lifestyle. The diet encourages eating an array of nutrient-dense, flavorful foods that can aid in natural oxidative processes, decrease aches and pains associated with inflammation and boost overall health and well-being.

While there is no rulebook for dieting, this cookbook does not advocate fad diet trends or unsustainable weight loss methods. We present our findings based on extensive research so you can make an informed decision that works best for your medical needs, genetic blueprint, budget, and goals.

When it comes to keeping fit, your goal should be to stay as active and healthy as possible. And if weight loss is also one of your long-term goals, then you want to focus on shedding excess pounds and maintaining a healthy lifestyle more broadly. Remember that your health will always come first and foremost before anything else, no matter what kind of diet or lifestyle change goals you're trying to achieve!

Printed in Great Britain
by Amazon

16112316R00047